DATE DUE

AMERICAN SOCIOLOGY SERIES

KIMBALL YOUNG, GENERAL EDITOR

AMERICAN SOCIOLOGY SERIES

Edited by KIMBALL YOUNG

THE COMMUNITY AND SOCIETY
AN INTRODUCTION TO SOCIOLOGY
By LORAN D. OSBORN
Los Angeles Institute of Family Relations,
and
MARTIN H. NEUMEYER
University of Southern California

CURRENT SOCIAL PROBLEMS
By JOHN M. GILLETTE
University of North Dakota,
and
JAMES M. REINHARDT
University of Nebraska

JUVENILE PROBATION
By BELLE BOONE BEARD
Sweet Briar College

AN INTRODUCTORY SOCIOLOGY
By KIMBALL YOUNG
University of Wisconsin

SOURCE BOOK FOR SOCIOLOGY
By KIMBALL YOUNG
University of Wisconsin

AMERICAN SOCIOLOGY SERIES

JUVENILE PROBATION

*An Analysis of the Case Records of Five Hundred
Children Studied at the Judge Baker Guidance Clinic and Placed on Probation
in the Juvenile Court of Boston*

BY

BELLE BOONE BEARD, PH.D.

*Associate Professor of Sociology, Sweet Briar College,
Sweet Briar, Virginia*

AMERICAN BOOK COMPANY

NEW YORK · CINCINNATI · CHICAGO · BOSTON · ATLANTA

FOREWORD

The fundamentally interesting fact concerning this book by Miss Beard is that it represents a sincere and capable attempt to find out what can be done for delinquents on probation.

For long years we have perceived the great values that might accrue through a careful assay of what has been and what can be accomplished by active probation for juveniles. Probation, like many another social institution, was established on the basis of a finely humane and practically valuable ideal, but without provision being made for well-considered growth and development. Indeed, the progress of probation from its earlier and later sound conceptions of justice and economies can largely be characterized as blundering ahead. Mr. Chute, of the National Probation Association, who has reason to know the state of affairs in his field, places himself on record by asserting that, in general, probation service is ineffectively organized, is not on a professional basis, and that all studies of results heretofore have been limited and inadequate. Can anyone doubt, then, that a soundly based inquiry into the methods and accomplishments of probation is highly pertinent?

Taken as a whole, probation is an important social institution. There are in this country more than four thousand probation officers and certainly there must be many more than a hundred thousand individuals on probation. Probation as social service is a going concern with much to its credit, but its methods as well as its accomplishments have never been clearly delineated. As a matter of fact, the term probation means almost anything, but we choose to believe that the essential

v

meaning of probation is active helpfulness—a well-founded attempt to adjust the individual, as Judge Hoffman says, to his peculiar situation in life. Any fair study of probation can only be of measures attempted as related to ends accomplished.

We heartily welcomed the advent of Miss Beard into our local situation. It seemed likely that as an unprejudiced outsider, trained in sociology, she could delve into the factual material of conditions, methods, and outcomes and bring to the surface valuable correlations of effort with accomplishment. Miss Beard proved to be a highly conscientious, painstaking worker who was able to enlist the services not only of some special investigators but also of other workers in the field, who freely gave their efforts to gathering data for her during the year that she actually spent here and later as further data were obtainable.

Since so many sources of information were available, it seems that the conclusions embodied in this study are sound. No doubt if a larger organization of a research staff had been possible, a few more facts would have been forthcoming, but it is the opinion of those who were in direct contact with Miss Beard that the investigative work was carefully conducted and that there is no reason to cavil at her statements of outcomes.

It must be conceded at once that with the immensely rapid alterations in our social conditions and situations, such as may make for greater or less production of delinquency and whole careers of crime, it is quite impossible from the findings of any given period to predict what the outcomes would be in a series of probation cases ten years later. We recognize this very clearly ourselves through noting the effects of the general use of automobiles, of the aftermaths of the war, or of the growing influence of moving pictures. The changing situation is similarly emphasized by Donham in *Business Adrift*, where it is made plain that because of frequently shifting conditions produced by new inventions and new methods business stabilities vanish. Essential human nature may remain the same, but influences molding the expression of natural tendencies, for better or worse, show great fluctuations. Any probation officer of long experience can tell of new situations that have to be combated every few years, and the question for him is always the availability of new weapons or newly sharpened old weapons with which to assail newly emerging dangerous forces. The best efforts of the probation officer of today in Boston, for example, do not altogether follow the lines of 1924 when most of the delinquents of this study were seen in court.

And so far as the case records of the Judge Baker Foundation, now the Judge Baker Guidance Center, are concerned, it should be stated, too, that we hope and believe that our methods of study of cases have vastly improved since 1924. With longer years of experience there have been changing emphases, particularly in the direction of attempting to know and understand better the deeper emotional attitudes that in not a few cases form the basic sources of delinquent trends. Good probation work will inevitably have more and more to meet these less superficial issues.

Just now I find opportunity to measure Miss Beard's achievement by the yardstick of an expert who surveys the field of probation from the standpoint of evaluating results. In a very recent article Bennet Mead, statistician of the Federal Bureau of Prisons, states that one of the principal functions of his division is to test results scientifically. Probation is to be evaluated (1) in terms of analysis of probation procedures; (2) through compilation of mass statistics of probation work; and (3), most important, by utilization of the case study method, the individual becoming the unit of evaluation. Indeed "the real efficiency of the probation department or officer should be judged from the degree of success attained in the social rehabilitation of the individual offender." Mead also insists that the task is one for the outside expert; the case study method is essential for truly scientific evaluation and it is to be supplemented by a progress record. In other words, unless account is taken of the offender's mental and physical equipment, his reactive tendencies, and his total background, no safe conclusions can be drawn concerning the efficacies of probation. Accumulation of mass statistics that fail to classify types of human material and types of backgrounds apparently seems to Mr. Mead, as it does to us, only a meaningless jumble of figures.

Miss Beard has used the case study and the record of progress. She has done more than take account of the physical and mental status of the offender; she has kept her eyes steadily upon the factors of causation and how these have been met or have not been met by active treatment under probation. It boils down to this: Her study is really a study of five hundred delinquents—partly selected in Court for study at the Clinic because they seemed to present the most difficult problems— and what happened to them on probation. It is not a study of the total amount of probation undertaken by the Boston Juvenile Court during the time; that, again, without case studies would mean largely the adding together of dissimilars.

When studying even superficially the results of probation and the procedures actually carried out on probation the reader should bear in mind possible differences between probation officers, differences in personality equipment, special training and energy, differences in their respective case loads, and in the districts in which they work. But the obviously difficult correlation of treatment and outcomes with such personality, executive, and geographical variations is far beyond the scope of this undertaking, although any intensive study of the work of any special court would have to determine whether or not such factors were fairly measurable.

By the case study method the evaluation of treatment on probation in terms of accomplishment, failure, possibilities or impossibilities, is difficult because of the variables involved. First, there is the delinquent himself with his particular physical and mental make-up, some elements of which may play a part in the production of delinquency. Certain of these elements would, of course, be considered matters of prime importance by those who hold that delinquency springs mainly from innate predispositions. But the individual as he exists at any given moment, with his particular reactive tendencies, is much more than a mass of innate predispositions; he has been conditioned by his life experiences. What can be known about the latter is of deepest concern to those who would understand the causes of delinquency and deal with them. Also the special circumstances that surrounded the individual at or near the time the delinquency was committed form part of the picture that has to be recognized if treatment is to be directed effectively towards prevention of repetition of offenses. And, finally, it is important to know what tools are at the disposal of the probation officer, what educational and recreational centers, what clinics, churches, clubs, Big Brother organizations, and what child helping agencies he can utilize. All these and still other factors play a part in the result—together they present a formidable array of variables to correlate with accomplishment.

Acknowledging the necessary shortcomings of any such study, it nevertheless stands out clearly that Miss Beard has produced a valuable estimate of the possibilities of probation, accomplished or not accomplished, under conditions that are by no means ideal, but which in some respects can be seen to rate favorably as compared with what obtains in most American communities. The study serves to call attention mainly to the types of causative factors which are modifiable, as shown by successful manipulation in many cases. Despite the failures, for reasons that are not always clear, it is thus obvious that much more reconstruction of delinquent tendencies is within the bounds of possibility than was formerly supposed.

The lapse of five years between the appearance of the offender in court and the time of the follow-up is a matter that of itself involves many considerations. Among these are the continuance or perpetuation of causations of which Miss Beard speaks. Then there is the introduction of new elements into the situation which might have made the individual an offender even if he had never offended previously. These partly account for the recidivism which occurred all too frequently. During this length of time, also, one would naturally expect outbreaks on the part of the offenders who showed abnormalities in emotional reactions or deep-set mental conflicts—those for whom no scientific treatment has as yet been provided.

We are led here once again to emphasize the matter that should be of gravest concern to society, namely, the prevention and checking of delinquency in order to head off criminal careers that spring from these beginnings. There are two main plans for waging a preventive battle: first, struggling understandingly and scientifically with those who are already delinquent and, second, assailing the features of social life which make for delinquency. Both are vastly important, but the success of the former depends upon the latter. Many phases of community life present forces too great for the probation officer to combat or for the delinquent to withstand. Until there is action over a wide front against these influences, much of the work of probation is bound to be a failure. Society will have to cure itself before it can cure delinquency.

WILLIAM HEALY

Judge Baker Guidance Center, Boston
January, 1934

ACKNOWLEDGMENTS

The author wishes to thank the following publishers for permission to quote from their publications:

ALFRED A. KNOPF, INC. For extracts from Cabot's Foreword to *500 Criminal Careers* (S. and E. Glueck), and from *Reconstructing Behavior in Youth* (Healy, Bronner, Baylor and Murphy).

THE ANNALS of the American Academy of Political and Social Science. For an extract from "The Significance of Mental Hygiene in Child Guidance" (Dr. Bernard Glueck), Vol. 121.

NATIONAL PROBATION ASSOCIATION, INC. For an extract from an article by Judge Charles W. Hoffman in *National Probation Proceedings for 1928*.

THE NEW REPUBLIC. For an extract from an article by Dr. William Healy in *The Child, the Clinic, and the Court*.

TABLE OF CONTENTS

LIST OF TABLES

SUPPLEMENTARY GRAPHS AND TABLES

(APPENDIX E)

List of Tables

CHAPTER I

INTRODUCTION

Juvenile probation has been aptly called the "forerunner" of the juvenile court movement. It was practiced in Massachusetts as early as 1830, and was sanctioned by statute in 1878. When the first juvenile court was established in 1899, probation became its recognized handmaiden. Since then its use has grown rapidly. State after state has incorporated it into its machinery for dealing with offenders. The exponents of probation reasoned as follows: apprehend the child when he first shows signs of delinquency; supervise him so that additional offenses will not be committed; prevent the development of criminal habits and attitudes, then there can be no crime.

Throughout the last thirty years a great deal has been written on the subject of probation. Some writers have dealt with the theoretical aspects of probation and others with practical problems, such as legal requirements, the training of probation officers, and methods of treatment. In this literature praises abound, and criticisms and doubts are rare, if not exceptional, and where they do exist they are directed toward technicalities rather than toward fundamental principles. But measurements of the effects of probation are lacking. Healy, Bronner, Baylor and Murphy, in the Introduction to *Reconstructing Behavior in Youth*,[1] have called attention already to this failure to consider results. They say:

"We have consistently stressed the fact that a great deal of work which goes under the name of social service and is initiated by people of humane tendencies is continued mainly because of the

[1] See p. 5. Reprinted from *Reconstructing Behavior in Youth*, by Healy, Bronner, Baylor and Murphy, by permission of and special arrangement with Alfred A. Knopf, Inc., authorized publishers.

momentum it has achieved rather than because it is thought that results are being accomplished. Curiously little evaluation of achievement is typical of much of the social work now being carried on; many social agencies not of a critical turn of mind, show no apparent interest in the results of their labors. This seems to be particularly true of courts and other organizations dealing with children."

WHAT IS JUVENILE PROBATION?

Judges, probation officers, and social workers have emphasized the possibilities of probation and have shown its efficacy in individual cases. But no authority has answered satisfactorily the imperative questions: What is probation treatment? What can it accomplish? Does it eliminate delinquency and prevent its recurrence?

Probation is a nebulous term. To many persons it is a vague concept somewhat synonymous to "given another chance" or "put under supervision." "Put on probation" when pronounced as the judge's decision does not carry with it the clear-cut meaning of "$5.00 fine" or "ten days in the county jail." Probation is not a sentence but is equivalent to a suspended sentence. Probation does not imply a prescribed program but probation treatment essentially means treatment fitted to the needs of the child.

Probation in this sense gives the offender a chance to make a satisfactory social adjustment. By avoiding either the stigma of incarceration or the freedom of acquittal, probation treatment gives opportunity for developing self-control with protection from unwise use of personal freedom. In the words of Judge Charles W. Hoffman:

"The essence of probation is helpfulness—the adjustment of the individual to his peculiar situation in life. . . . Probation is not vindictive. It is charitable in all its implications. Its aim is to save those upon whom the burdens of life bear heavily and who without help and guidance might be lost. Had it not been for the existence of probation for some twenty years previous to the year 1899, and had not other states and communities followed the lead of Massachusetts in probation, we would have had no juvenile courts today. Probation suggested the idea of eliminating the criminal process in the treatment of children. . . . Were it not that today probation is accepted as a sound and sane judicial policy, there would be no accredited approach to the solution of the problem of crime of which we hear so much in our civil life. It is impossible to work along any other line today than that of discovering the origin and causes of anti-social conduct in all its relationships." [2]

Formality in dealing with juvenile delinquents was eliminated in order that a friendly personal relationship might be established between the probation officer and the child. It is a fundamental principle underlying the juvenile court that the juvenile offender is considered as an unadjusted individual who must be protected and helped to the attainment of his best capabilities—not as a criminal who must be punished or "reformed." In what respects, then, is the work of the probation officer different from the work of other persons dealing with problem children? Does the probation officer use a specific technique which can be distinguished from that of the visiting teacher and the family case worker? Is the approach of the probation officer to the boy who has stolen money different from that of the parent or of the school principal in meeting the same problem? To what extent does the probation officer dictate the conduct of the child or restrict his activities? Does the probation officer attend personally to all the needs of the child or does he work through existing social agencies?

In order to answer these and other related questions this investigation was undertaken. The Judge Baker Foundation was chosen as the place for this study because of the excellent coöperation between this Clinic and the Boston Juvenile Court. In 1929, when the study was started, the Judge Baker Foundation had already been closely connected with this Court for eleven years. During this time the Court had sent 3266 cases to the Clinic for examination in order that experts might

[2] Hoffman, Charles W., *National Probation Proceedings*, 1928, p. 12.

recommend the kind of treatment that seemed best fitted to the needs of each delinquent.[3]

While only about one-third of all the children dealt with by the Court were sent to the Clinic for examination, this number includes the majority of the children believed to present difficult behavior or personality problems. Probation was the treatment prescribed for about one-half of the cases studied for the Court. They offer unusual advantages as source material.

In the first place, Massachusetts was a pioneer state in probation practice. The Boston Juvenile Court had, for a quarter of a century, profited by the leadership of two judges renowned for their social vision.[4] The records of this court are kept more accurately, more consistently, and more fully than the average juvenile court records. Furthermore, the turnover of the staff of probation officers is low. In fact, almost all of the 500 delinquents studied here had been supervised

[3] Hereafter in this study "the Clinic" may be interpreted as meaning the Judge Baker Foundation: "Boston's Center for the Guidance of Childhood and Youth," and "the Court" may be interpreted as referring to the "Boston Juvenile Court." The Judge Baker Foundation gave the writer the opportunity to make this study because this Clinic felt the need of scientific information regarding the technique and results of probation. A detailed outline of the investigation was made with the assistance of Dr. William Healy and Dr. Augusta Bronner, Directors of the Judge Baker Foundation, and of Judge Frederick Cabot, Mr. W. J. Bell, Chief Probation Officer, and Mr. Hans Weiss, Probation Officer, of the Boston Juvenile Court. The analysis of the data was made under the supervision of Professor Susan M. Kingsbury, Director of the Carola Woerishoffer Graduate Department of Social Economy and Social Research. Miss Almena Dawley, Lecturer in Social Economy and Social Research in the same department, helped in supervising the study. The tremendous task of securing and verifying data and of making follow-up visits to the homes of the 500 children was made possible only by the untiring assistance of the employees and volunteer workers of the Judge Baker Foundation. Miss Mildred Dewey, Head of Social Service, of the Judge Baker Foundation, assisted in securing follow-up reports and in facilitating the process of the investigation; also Miss Amy Hamburger, Miss Elizabeth Waterman and Miss Elizabeth Fowler gave generously of their time and energy in volunteer service. A score or more of students from the Simmons College School of Social Work, the Department of Social Ethics of Harvard University, and the Departments of Sociology and Psychology of Boston University rendered valuable volunteer service in collecting and recording information. The entire manuscript was read and many valuable suggestions were made by Dr. Healy and Dr. Bronner and by Dr. Myra E. Shimberg, Research Associate of the Judge Baker Foundation. The study was accepted by the Faculty of Bryn Mawr College as a dissertation in fulfillment of the requirements for the degree of Doctor of Philosophy.

[4] Judge Harvey Humphrey Baker in whose memory the Judge Baker Foundation was organized, and Judge Frederick P. Cabot, nationally and internationally recognized as an authority on the treatment of juvenile delinquency. (Chairman of the Committee on Delinquency of the 1930 White House Conference on Child Health and Child Welfare.)

by officers who were still in the same positions or who were available for consultation. In addition to experience, long tenure of office had given to these officers a vast accumulation of knowledge regarding family and neighborhood groups and their peculiar traits and reactions, which enabled them to judge the results of their treatment more accurately than would have been possible with a changing staff.

In the second place, the Judge Baker Foundation records afford unusual advantages. The Clinic was organized and is directed by Dr. William Healy and Dr. Augusta Bronner, pioneers in the movement for the individual treatment of offenders—a method that bases treatment on the needs and possibilities of the individual child.[5] Although the procedure of child guidance clinics is still in a state of flux and is being constantly revised, it was nevertheless at that period no longer a wholly new venture, but was founded upon several years of experience in Chicago.

The third advantage in the case material as a source arises from the excellent spirit of goodwill and coöperation existing between both the Court and the Clinic and other social agencies of the city and state. Chief among the agencies contributing valuable information for the study were the Massachusetts Probation Commission and the Social Service Exchange. Massachusetts keeps a permanent record of the arrests and Court appearances of both juvenile and adult offenders. The extensive files of the Massachusetts Probation Commission furnish information regarding occupation and present address of offenders as well as their entire delinquency records. These data were especially helpful in locating recidivists for follow-up visits.[6]

The Social Service Index, the clearing house for all social welfare agencies, supplies data concerning all contacts made by any member of the child's family with any social agency.

[5] Healy, William, *The Individual Delinquent.*
[6] The Commissioner of Probation, Mr. Herbert Parsons, rendered service to the investigator by giving liberally of his time for conference as well as by allowing frequent consultation of the records of court appearances and disposition of the children studied and of their families.

Family case work agencies, child welfare agencies, health agencies, settlement houses and clubs, without exception, coöperated graciously by allowing the use of their records and by assisting in investigations whenever they were requested to do so.

The 500 cases chosen for this study appeared serially at the Judge Baker Foundation beginning January 1, 1924. This number was chosen for two reasons: it furnished sufficiently large major classifications to warrant statistical treatment; it comprised the work of more than two years, eliminating any fluctuations in type of problem or type of treatment which short-time intervals might yield.[7] January 1, 1924, was decided upon as a date sufficiently distant to allow for a post-probation period in which to observe the effects of probation. Follow-up interviews were begun January 1, 1929, giving an interval of approximately five years since probation began.

In order that all records might be uniform, only cases examined at the Judge Baker Foundation are included.[8] This factor may or may not have resulted in a selected group. Clinical analysis was advised whenever the Court wished fuller information regarding the physical, mental, and emotional make-up of the child. Selection was not made on the basis of offense; indeed, no objective criteria have been consistently followed. Certain types of cases demand specialized treatment prescribed by statute; others need skilled individual programs. The following cases were usually sent to the Clinic: children who were suspected of being mentally deficient; those considered serious offenders; those who seem to present physical, mental, educational, vocational, or personality difficulties; or those where the parent-child's relationship appeared difficult.

[7] Since less than one-half of all children appearing in the Court are sent for clinical study, these cases do not represent the entire work of the Probation Officer.

[8] A description of the procedure of the Boston Juvenile Court and a brief statement of the work of the Judge Baker Foundation are found in the Judge Baker Foundation Publication Number 1, *Harvey Humphrey Baker: Upbuilder of the Juvenile Court.* More detailed description of the work of the Clinic and of its relationship to the Court and to other social agencies is given in Judge Baker Foundation Publication Number 2, *Judge Baker Foundation Case Studies, Series I,* 1923.

ASSEMBLING THE DATA

Upon the schedule was recorded material appearing in the records of the Court, Clinic, and coöperating agencies listed above.[9] Where the Court records did not give complete information, the probation officers were consulted and in almost every instance were able to supply the desired details either from their own notes or from memory. They were especially helpful in obtaining reports on present location and activities, since in many cases they had continued informal contacts long after probation officially ended. All cases were cleared by the Massachusetts Probation Commission and by the Social Service Index. If a case-working agency was actively working with the family, the visitor was consulted before a follow-up call was made. In some cases the visitor secured all information desired for this investigation, in other cases the visitor coöperated with the investigator in making appointments with the children studied. In all other cases home visits were made to secure the child's history since probation ended. Great care and tact were exercised in making follow-up visits and in securing information from relatives and friends. Often as many as ten visits were made to secure the desired information.

These voluminous records have been analyzed in this study in order to answer for those dealing with juvenile offenders very practical questions regarding probation as a form of social treatment of delinquency. Since it is at the Court that the probation officer first meets his charges, a brief description of the court procedure follows.

In a progressive court utilizing the services of a child guidance clinic, the steps preliminary to probation might be described somewhat as follows: The reception room of the Juvenile Court is rapidly filled by children, escorted by questioning, incensed, or humiliated parents.[10]

[9] See Appendix B for schedule.
[10] The following case histories and all of those cited hereafter have been drawn from the records of the Court, the Clinic, and the investigation, using the same terminology as there appears, so far as it could be done. Wherever it seemed necessary, the situation was disguised. All names are fictitious and all identifying information has been altered.

Mrs. M. shows her annoyance at the whole procedure by a re-vengeful twist of Johnny's ear and by turning down his collar with the well known gesture which means that the owner of the collar must try to be decent, but which adds that the parent scarcely expects him to be.

Mrs. Q. is indignant that Percy, who is always such a good, quiet, little boy, should be brought to Court. She is not interested in hearing the charge against him; she is very certain that he is not guilty. Percy in the meantime has surreptitiously placed the stolen ring in the pocket of a Negro man sitting beside him.

Mr. X. looks anxiously at Herman, six feet tall, who has told him repeatedly that he has no intention of working and that he will punch out his father's eyes if he reports him to Court. For three years Mr. X. has threatened to report Herman, but because of his wife's tears desisted, yielding to his son's demands for money and submitting to his abuse. It would be difficult to say which is more frightened by the ordeal of appearing in Court or which is more anxious regarding the outcome—the cringing father or the bully of a son. Will this only make the home situation more intolerable? Can the Court make Herman change his attitude? The mother doesn't want him sent away, she could not bear the "disgrace"; "Couldn't the judge just scare him—put some starch in him and make him get a job and help support the large family?"

Little Fanny B. is pale and trembling as she timidly enters the courtroom alone. Her thin sweater is drawn tightly around her soiled, ragged dress, which hangs in folds on her slender body. When asked where her mother is, Fanny hesitates, and finally replies that she is ill. The probation officer knows that the mother is probably too intoxicated to appear in answer to the summons.

In a friendly manner the judge, the parent, and the child talk over the situation and the problems involved. In a great number of cases, as previously stated, the judge postpones his decision until the children are examined by the Clinic.

At the Clinic the delinquent's parents are interviewed by the social worker who secures from them a detailed account of the background of the child, his developmental, health, and school history, his interests, habits, emotional life, personality characteristics, and family attitudes.

Meanwhile the delinquent is given a series of examinations. The psychologist by means of a battery of standardized tests determines his mental status and his special abilities and disabilities. The doctor gives him a physical examination. The psychiatrist obtains an "own story" in order to get the delinquent's point of view and his ideation, his emotional reactions and the underlying causes of his difficulty. Based on the information thus gleaned, the Clinic makes a diagnosis of the child's problem and general or specific recommendations for his treatment. These recommendations, while not compulsory, are usually accepted by the Court and form a basis for the operations of the probation officer. Consequently, in this Court, the extent to which the Clinic recommendations have been carried out has proven to be an excellent criterion by which the results of probation treatment may be measured.

Before the child's next visit to the Court the judge has a complete summary of these findings and recommendations which he may use in his disposition of the case. The judge then places the child in the care of the probation officer to whom he has been assigned.

At this time the child is counseled concerning his behavior and is in some cases given a written statement outlining the conditions of his probation. For example, in the Boston Juvenile Court, each child is given a report card that is kept by the child and signed by the probation officer each time the child reports to him. The reverse side of the card bears the minimum conditions of probation, stated as follows:

BOSTON JUVENILE COURT

To ——————————

The Court has put you on probation to give you a chance to make good. You must do your best to succeed in school and at work, at home, in church or temple, and among your friends.

If you are making good, the Court will end your probation. If you are not, the Court may send you away to be trained.

Your time on probation is until ——————————. The Court may make it shorter or longer.

HOW TO WIN ON PROBATION

1. Keep yourself clean in body, mind, and habits and win health, strength, and courage.
2. Keep good hours at meals in the day and at night and win regular ways of living.
3. Keep friendly and helpful with your father, mother, brothers and sisters and win their pride in you and a better home.
4. Keep active in games and clubs and win good sportsmanship.
5. Keep good company with friends and books and win an idea of what can be done in the world.
6. Keep good attendance at every session of school and win a high mark for effort.
7. Keep at work for regular hours every day and win a place for yourself.
8. Keep strictly your religious duties and win reverence and faith.
9. Keep the law and the rules of the city and win as a good citizen.

METHODS USED BY THE PROBATION OFFICER

The probation officer's job is to give guidance to boys and girls who may or may not recognize the need of advice or assistance. His field of labor covers situations caused by the failure of someone else—the failure of the child to live up to the expectations of his parents or to the standards of conduct demanded by society; the failure of parents to provide protection and guidance; or the failure of society to insure adequate environmental conditions. It is sufficient to say that something has gone wrong. The situation that confronts the officer has the appearance of a crisis, even though it may have been gradually developing for a long time. Delinquency involves emotional as well as intellectual ramifications. The mere fact of court appearance often causes a defensive attitude on the part of the family, fear and antagonism on the part of the child, and sensitiveness, tension, and embarrassment for all.

The probation officer must enter this arena of struggling emotions and bring order out of chaos. He must bring about the best possible solution of the delinquent's problems. Perhaps this will involve guiding a child through a crisis which will require his efforts for only a few weeks. Perhaps he must help the child to develop a new philosophy of life and set in operation this philosophy—a task requiring many months.

How can such changes be brought about? What is the probation officer's *entrée?* Dr. Cabot, in his Foreword to *500 Criminal Careers* by Sheldon and Eleanor Glueck, says:

"So far as I have seen such reforms or heard of them from others, there has been at least one necessary condition: that someone should come to know and to understand the man in so intimate and friendly a way that he comes to a better understanding of himself and to a truer comprehension of the world he lives in." [11]

The dynamic emotional relationship existing between the probation officer and the child differs from that of case worker and client. In the latter case assistance is requested. The client recognizes a need. In probation the client not only may not ask for help but may even resent the appearance of the probation officer. He is likely to regard the probation officer as a force to be combated or an enemy to be feared. Obviously a different treatment technique is needed. As a preparation for the new alliance, the judge explains the meaning of probation. The child is told that he is in need of supervision and is assured that the probation officer is a friend who will stand ready to help him. But since the court and all persons connected with it have always connoted to him "punishment," the child is not likely to look forward with any pleasure to this friendship.

The good probation officer tries to dispel fear in the first interview by showing that his job is not to punish, but to understand the problem of the child. An officer may achieve this result by saying "I want to hear your side of this story, so I can speak to the Judge for you." The child usually has some conception of a court of law and considers this equivalent to having a lawyer plead his case. But more often instead of encouraging the child to believe "I'm on your side"—a belief which later may lead to disappointment—the probation officer

[11] See p. ix. Reprinted from *500 Criminal Careers*, by Sheldon and Eleanor Glueck, by permission of and special arrangement with Alfred A. Knopf, Inc., authorized publishers.

seeks to establish a status of neutrality. The officer shows his sympathy and interest by listening to the child's story. He is never too busy to hear a tale of woe from his little client. He respects the personal opinions and feelings of the child and protects his secrets from listening ears. Later in the course of treatment the confidential nature of interviews is emphasized.

The probation officer may win the confidence of the child by interpreting him and his needs to his parents. He reviews in the presence of both the child's life situation, bringing into their normal position factors that have been exaggerated. This method is especially efficacious where the demands of the parents exceed the abilities of the child, whether these relate to grades in school, obedience to parents themselves, employment, or social adjustment.

The probation officer plans outings, parties, and entertainments to ingratiate himself with his charges. His services include many deeds of kindness and thoughtfulness belonging in the realm of friendship—such as taking small gifts of toys, flowers, or books to sick children, or sending tickets to free performances of theatre or movie.

Aside from any therapeutic value to be derived, the probation officer establishes rapport by showing a lively and permanent interest in the events of the child's daily life—in the grade Earl made on that History test that he dreaded, in whether Susan's grandmother approved of the new hat she bought, in the new baby that just arrived at Nadia's house, and in Pat's father's losing his job.

The probation officer is especially careful that his visit must mean to the child increased opportunity for self-expression, rather than the thwarting of his desires. For example:

Miss B., who is supervising Ella, meets her in a department store, shopping. Ella is accompanied by a girl somewhat older and much more neatly dressed than herself. Ella, feeling certain that Miss B. will not betray her relationship, eagerly introduces her new friend. She is acting upon Miss B.'s suggestion that she try to make friends with the more attractive girls in her factory and cease chumming with her neighbor Madge who taught her shoplifting; and Ella is anxious for approval. Miss B., who is herself charmingly dressed, is interested in Edith and converses pleasantly with both girls. They separate well pleased—Miss B. that Ella is improving in her choice of companions, and Edith, that her new friend has status as shown by the reactions of a stylish and cultured person, Miss B. But what is of most significance is that Ella is pleased with the encounter. She has increased her own prestige in the eyes of Edith. Her self-respect has risen several degrees. And her confidence in her probation officer has been strengthened. They are partners in the game of life. If Miss B. had handled the situation less skillfully and exclaimed, "Oh, I'm so glad to see you, Ella. I want you to report to me at the Court at eleven o'clock Monday instead of at ten," all would have been lost. Even though Edith had not acted very differently, the effect upon Ella might have been disastrous. If she has not told Edith of her escapade and of her probation (and the chances are nine to one that she hasn't), she will feel humiliated, or annoyed, or at least thwarted.

In summary, the probation officer's ability to establish a friendly relationship depends upon first, his personality; second, the resources at his command; and third, his professional skill and technique. Under the first heading come: an unaffected fundamental interest in human beings and also tact, humor, insight, and mental alertness. Neatness and style in personal appearance are decided assets when working with adolescents.

In the second place, ample time to devote to each case is essential. No matter how many desirable personality traits and how much professional skill a probation officer possesses, he cannot bring about reforms in a person whom he has no time to see. The extent to which the probation officer can obtain new experiences for the child depends upon the available resources. The use made by the probation officer of settlements, clubs, hospitals, parks, employment agencies, visiting teachers, and case workers is shown in the chapters dealing with specific types of treatment.

The professional skill which is the result of experience in applying knowledge comes largely through practice. It involves more than the mechanical manipulation of interviews and visits so that the largest number of persons can be seen under the most propitious circumstances, in the least amount of time, and with the least expenditure of money—though that itself is important. It means a technique for the proper distribution of praise and blame; for seeing and commenting upon or for ignoring actions, attitudes, and moods; for assisting, encouraging, and suggesting solutions, or for demanding that the child think through his own problems depending upon the needs of the individual case.

This is perhaps an idealized picture of probation, for it certainly does not describe probation work as it appears throughout the country, not even in this Court.

Probation technique will perhaps evolve as a combination of the techniques used by case workers, educators, club leaders, parents, and friends. Countless quotations could be selected from the records studied indicating that the probation officer seemed to have a technique peculiar to his profession. Paul's comments are illustrative:

"Mr. White always pops up whenever I go over to Wall Street. He saw me just as I was starting in the Pool Room, and I was sure scared, for he told me last week he'd have to send me up if I didn't stay away from there. What do you think he did? He slaps me on the arm like as if he was a pal and says, 'How about going swimming with me tonight?' There was something in the push of his voice that made me feel I'd be digging my own grave if I didn't go. But when I looked at him I see a smile that made me feel that swimming was the very thing I had been wanting to do all my life, and I was glad he had thought of it. He's like that. He says things you never would 'a thought of alone, but the way he says 'em makes you think you had the idea first. And when you tell him about how it is at home and what a mess your family is in, he never laughs the way the gang does. When Pop was in jail he didn't act high hat and shocked. You would 'a thought his pop was in jail too, the way he understood and talked about it."

CHAPTER II

500 DELINQUENTS AND THEIR PROBLEMS

Before attempting treatment the probation officer should know all that he can about the delinquent. The intensive study of each individual described in the preceding chapter revealed a multiplicity of detail. These data may be divided for practical purposes into two classes: first, the unmodifiable data concerning the delinquent at the time he appears in court; and second, those aspects of the child's life with which the probation officer is chiefly concerned in treatment. The latter type of material—dealing with the home situation, physical condition, recreation and companionship, work and education of the child—is reserved for succeeding chapters discussing treatment and comprising the major part of this book.

The former type of information includes age, sex, intelligence, nationality, religion, home status, offense, causation, and programs for treatment. This statistical material tends to answer the questions so often asked: "Are boys more likely to be delinquent than girls?" "Is it only the feeble-minded who get into court?" "Are most juvenile offenders foreigners?" "Do not delinquents usually come from broken homes?" "What is the relation of poverty to crime?" "What offense is most often committed?" The clinical study tends to answer the questions: "Why do children become delinquents?" and "What can be done with the youthful offender?"

SEX

The 500 children with whom this study deals are four-fifths boys.[1] This distribution cannot be considered indicative

[1] When taken serially the first 500 cases included 104 girls and 396 boys. Since this number so nearly approached a four to one ratio, the last four girls were arbitrarily

of the relative goodness or badness of boys and girls. Nor can it be interpreted as indicating that four times as many boys as girls need probation. It means only that, of the children sent by the Court to the Judge Baker Foundation for study, four times as many boys as girls were placed on probation during this particular period of two and one-half years. The smaller number of girls on probation may be due to the demand of neighborhood standards that parents handle cases of delinquency among girls, while they appeal to the court for help in dealing with recalcitrant boys, or it may be due to custom that allows boys to wander about on the streets, while girls are kept closely at home. Differences in court procedure for boys and for girls, and in the attitudes of complainants toward delinquent girls may also reduce the number of the latter to be assigned this type of treatment.

Fundamentally, the two sexes have much the same forces motivating behavior whether these forces be called "instincts," "prepotent tendencies," "desire to function," or "determining tendencies." Due to cultural influences, however, the overt behavior of male and female children often takes quite unlike patterns. This variation in reaction is apparent in much of the discussion of causation and treatment of delinquency in subsequent chapters. More obvious differences will be seen in type of offense, in attitude toward anti-social acts, and in recreation habits. As a result, sex has been used throughout this study as a major classification.

AGE

The age limits of children to be placed on probation in the juvenile court are determined in advance by statute; the lower and upper limits in the court studied being seven and seventeen years respectively. On the basis of behavior problems, these ten years covering the possible probation period in the life of a child seem to break into three approximately equal divisions: the first from seven years to ten years, six months; the second from ten years, six months, to thirteen years, six

dropped and the next four boys added to the list in order to facilitate the statistical computations.

months; and the third from thirteen years, six months, to seventeen years. The first and last divisions cover periods of three and one-half years, while the second includes only three years.

TABLE I

Age distribution of 500 boys and girls on probation

Age	Boys		Girls		Total	
	Number	Per cent	Number	Per cent	Number	Per cent
7 years to 10 years 6 months............	69	17	5	5	74	15
10 years 6 months to 13 years 6 months....	133	34	24	24	157	31
13 years 6 months to 17 years............	198	49	71	71	269	54
Total................................	400	100	100	100	500	100

Table I shows that both boys and girls are found in greater numbers in the older age groups, but the relative distributions for the two sexes are quite dissimilar. The boys in this study are proportionately younger than the girls. Seventeen per cent of the boys are under ten years, six months, while only five per cent of the girls fall in this category.[2] This difference is also shown in the average ages of the two groups. The mean age of probation boys is thirteen years and three months, while the mean age of girls is fourteen years and four months.

NATIVITY AND RACE

Contrary to an opinion often expressed in the press and on the lecture platform, less than one-tenth of these 500 delinquents were foreign born (9 per cent of the boys and 10 per cent of the girls). Twenty-one of the foreign born came from Italy, nine from Canada and the remaining seventeen from eleven other countries. All but five had lived in Boston over five years. The remaining nine-tenths were native born. More than half of the total number were born in Boston (59 per

[2] Unless otherwise stated, statistical differences that are interpreted as significant have been tested by Hart's Reliability of Percentage Tables. See Hart, Hornell, "The Reliability of a Percentage," *Journal of American Statistical Association*, March, 1926.

cent of the boys and 45 per cent of the girls) , and an additional number (23 per cent of the boys and 32 per cent of the girls) were born in other cities of Massachusetts. That is, more than three-fourths are natives of the state.

The more important question is not where the child was born, but under what influences he has been reared. Immigrants, especially those who live in foreign districts and do not have close contact with native American citizens, perpetuate their own food habits and customs of dress, language, religious observance, and commercial practice. The child born and reared under such circumstances has to some extent a "foreign background" similar to that of the child born in Russia, China, or Italy.

But one-fifth of the 1000 parents represented here were born in the United States. Also one-fifth came from the British Isles, Canada, or other English colonies, making a total of two-fifths from English-speaking countries. Approximately two-fifths were natives of southern Europe, chiefly of Italy and Sicily; and the remaining one-fifth were born in Russia, Poland, Lithuania, or other northern European countries. Only 6 per cent of the 500 children are colored, most of these being full-blooded Negroes born in the southern part of the United States.

Of the 300 parents to whom English was not the native tongue, only one-third have acquired this language. More men than women have learned to speak and write English, due presumably to their more frequent contacts outside the home and neighborhood. In more than one-fourth (27 per cent) of all the homes Italian, Polish, Yiddish, or Greek is used exclusively, while in many others foreign languages are used to some degree. This factor not only has a bearing upon the understanding of the habits and attitudes of the child, but also vitally affects the nature and extent of social treatment.

MENTALITY

The classification of general intelligence used in this study is the final estimate as reported on the Judge Baker Foundation Conference Summary. Although a Stanford-Binet test was given to each child, the score on this test alone was not used as a basis of classification. Diagnosis of general intelligence level was made on the basis of the sum total of a group of tests. For this reason the classification does not coincide exactly with the terminology used by Terman [3] and others; but for the purposes of prognosis the total used seemed to the Clinic to be of greater value. For example, one child, Simon Leitz, has an I.Q. of ninety-four according to the Binet scale, but when it was found that this score was accounted for to an unusual degree by a very high auditory memory span, and that he showed marked deficiencies in other tests, his general intelligence was classified as "fair" rather than as "good."

TABLE II

Distribution of 400 boys and 100 girls according to intelligence classification

	Boys		Girls		Total	
	Number	Per cent	Number	Per cent	Number	Per cent
Superior	28	7	13	13	41	8
Good	120	30	22	22	142	28
Fair	96	24	12	12	108	22
Poor	78	19	24	24	102	20
Defective	72	18	25	25	97	20
Unclassified	6	2	4	4	10	2
Total	400	100	100	100	500	100

Four-fifths of the total number tested have normal mentality, though one-fourth of this group fall in the category "poor" or what is termed by some psychologists "border zone" or "dull normal." Less than one-fifth can be called "defective."

[3] Terman, Lewis M., *The Measurement of Intelligence*, p. 79.

HOME STATUS

The most important factors in the home environment of the child are without question the presence or absence of parents, and the nature of their interest in, and control and supervision of their children. Of the 500 children, 144 boys (36 per cent) and 40 girls (40 per cent) come from broken homes.

"Broken home" is used here in a very broad sense to cover any home from which either one or both of the actual parents of the child is absent.

From the point of view of the child and his relationships the broken homes are of three types: (1) one or both parents are dead; (2) both parents are alive, but not living together; (3) the child is with adoptive or foster parents. About one-fourth of all the children (23 per cent of the boys and 25 per cent of the girls) fall in the first category and a smaller number (11 per cent of the boys and 13 per cent of the girls) in the second. Only seven children live with adoptive or foster parents.

The remaining homes, "normal" as to residence of both parents with the child, are by no means uniform in the quantity of oversight and guidance given. In sixty-two of these cases the mother as well as the father works away from home. In a few cases grandparents or older sisters supervise the younger children, but in the majority of them no mother substitute is provided.

The crucial factor, however, is not the absence or presence of parents, but the relationship existing between parent and child. An over-protective attitude on the part of parents may be more devastating than neglect or abuse. In the succeeding chapters of this study illustrations will be given of the many ways in which an inadequate parent-child relationship hampered the personality development of the child.

What is the economic status of the homes of juvenile delinquents? Four criteria are examined in an attempt to answer this question: (1) the Judge Baker Foundation Conference

Summary; (2) the average weekly wage of the family; (3) occupation of father; and (4) registration with a relief-giving agency. Four-fifths of the children come from homes where the pressure of economic need is felt, a third of them being at the poverty level. According to reports received from relief-giving agencies, 186 families were known to have received financial assistance.[4]

According to the Judge Baker Foundation economic classi-fication 20 per cent of the homes are rated "good," 40 per cent "fair," 38 per cent "poor" and 2 per cent "unknown." [5] The wage or salary income of the family was recorded in only 136 cases (34 per cent). For these, the mean weekly income is $27.52, and the median income, $24.40. The range of income reported is from $4.00 to $55.00 per week. More than fifty different occupations are recorded for the 333 fathers for whom this information is available. One father has a license to beg with a tin cup, another to play a hurdy-gurdy; one father claimed to be a priest, and another to be proprietor of a large hotel. For convenience, occupations are grouped under three descriptive categories, as follows: "White Collar," 34; "Skilled and Semi-skilled," 155; and "Unskilled," 144.[6]

OFFENSES

"Delinquent" is a legal term applied because of specific acts committed. These acts, or "offenses," are viewed by the Court as symptoms of the lack of adjustment to society, not as expressions of "innate wickedness" or lack of moral stamina. The word "offense," then, is not synonymous with "problem."

[4] These agencies included the Family Welfare Society, Overseers of the Poor and Mothers' Aid, the Provident Association, Federation of Jewish Charities, North End Catholic Guild, State Temporary Aid, International Institute, and Salvation Army Relief Department.

[5] "Good" is used to designate the home capable of self-maintenance on a standard of health and decency. "Fair" describes the home that normally has sufficient income to meet daily average needs, but must have outside assistance to meet emergencies. "Poor" applies to all homes in which the average income is inadequate for sub-sistence.

[6] "White Collar" includes all independent owners of businesses, managers, buyers, foremen and salaried clerks. "Skilled and Semi-skilled" includes bakers, laundrymen, blacksmiths, bricklayers, carpenters, and pressmen as well as skilled and semi-skilled workers in factories, foundries, mills, and machine-shops. "Unskilled" includes "day laborers" and all persons whose jobs require no previous training or experience.

But since the commitment of an offense is the objective evidence of an inner "problem," attention is often centered upon the overt act. It is significant, therefore, to see what kind of acts bring children into the hands of the law.

The offenses committed by these 500 juveniles range in apparent seriousness from taking an apple from a vender's cart or a box of matches from a five-and-ten-cent-store to forging checks for hundreds of dollars, stealing automobiles, professional prostitution, and safe-breaking with burglars' tools. In reality, however, offenses cannot be arbitrarily ranked in seriousness. The stealing of a penny by one child may be indicative of a greater degree of moral turpitude than the stealing of ten dollars by another child. Motive and intent, not intrinsic worth of goods purloined, determine the seriousness of the offense. There remains in society, however, a strong tendency to rank offenders according to their offenses. This attitude was shown in this investigation by parents who said, "I knew Mike would lie, but I never dreamed he'd steal. Well, you'll just have to send him away." The same lack of comprehension is shown by employers who say, "She ran away from home? Well, then, I can't hire her."

According to the Court nomenclature, nineteen different offenses are charged against boys and eleven against girls. These offenses, listed in Table IV (page 24), may be grouped according to the nature of the act into four categories, as shown in Table III.

Offense Against Property includes larceny, breaking and entering, larceny of automobile, receiving stolen goods, possessing burglars' tools, destroying property, and fire setting. More than three-fourths of all the boys' offenses and almost two-thirds of all the girls' offenses fall under this caption. In contrast to the small number of cases in which there was malicious mischief or destruction of property without any advantage accruing to the offender, are five times as many instances of purloining of goods for use. Of all the sixty-one charges of larceny by girls fifty-five were for shoplifting articles of clothing, jewelry, or accessories either for themselves and friends

TABLE III

Percentage distribution of boys and girls according to offense

	Percentage		
	Boys	Girls	Total
Offense Against Property...............	77	62	74
Offense Against Person..................	7	13	8
Runaway and Stubborn Complaints......	11	20	13
Petty Misdemeanors....................	5	5	5
Total...............................	100	100	100

or for members of their families. This type of offense bears close relation to economic need and also to the desire for adventure.

Two types of crimes resulting from uninhibited elemental desires are included under *Offenses Against Person,* the sex urge, and the tendency to use physical force for self-protection or for avenging an insult.

The charges represented in the categories *Runaway, Stubborn and Wayward Complaints* are of quite different origin from the two preceding classes. These are children who may or may not have committed any specific offense punishable by law, but who are reported by parents because of failure to obey them, or are picked up by the police, or are reported by others for being on the street late at night, or for refusing to go home. Almost twice as many girls as boys appear here, not because more girls than boys are guilty of these types of behavior, but because of the difference in community standards for the two sexes.

Under *Misdemeanors* are included such petty offenses as profanity, peddling in restricted territory or without a license, idle and disorderly conduct, and evading street-car fares and violating park rules. These do not injure the property or person of another, and yet interfere with the rights of others

and with general welfare to such an extent that they are prohibited by law.

TABLE IV

Offenses for which 400 boys and 100 girls were reported to the Boston Juvenile Court

Count	Number		
	Boys	Girls	Total
Larceny (excluding larceny of auto)......	136	61	197
Breaking and entering..................	117	0	117
Larceny of automobile..................	42	0	42
Runaway............................	25	9	34
Sex misconduct*	22	10	32
Wayward and stubborn complaints......	19	11	30
Petty misdemeanors**..................	21	3	24
Assault and battery	6	3	9
Destruction of property.................	6	0	6
Receiving stolen goods..................	2	1	3
Forgery	2	0	2
Possessing burglars' tools	2	0	2
Truancy	0	1	1
Drunkenness	0	1	1
Total..............................	400	100	500

* Includes lewd and licentious cohabitation, fornication, exposure, sexual assault, unnatural act, and abuse of female child.
** Includes peddling, trespassing, carrying weapons, fire setting, disturbing assembly, idle and disorderly conduct, violating park rules, profanity, and evading fares.

THE RELATION OF AGE AND NATIVITY TO TYPE OF OFFENSE

Only three types of offense bear a definite relation to age,
namely, larceny of automobile and "breaking and entering"
by boys, and sex misconduct by girls.

The stealing of automobiles is engaged in only by older

boys. Two obvious reasons present themselves, namely, the younger child would have had no experience in driving a car and would not know how to start a machine, and even if he did know how to drive, he could not have a license and would be immediately detected by police. This is the only boys' offense that was not committed by some one of each age group; it was not perpetrated by any boy under 10½ years, but in 88 per cent of the cases it was by boys over 13½ years old.

The charge of "breaking and entering" (unlike larceny, which was engaged in by both sexes of all ages), was listed most frequently for younger boys, 49 per cent of all the offenses of the younger age group falling here. These cases include chiefly excursions of crowds or gangs into neighborhood stores to get candy, food, and toys; breaking into vacant buildings to plunder or for a secret meeting place for the gang; and forced entrance into factories or mills prompted by curiosity and a desire for a thrill. As boys grow older they seem to discover that the rewards of this type of behavior do not warrant the risks of punishment involved. However, this group also includes some charges of "breaking and entering, and larceny" of which the older boys especially were guilty.

Sex misconduct of girls naturally is a problem of late adolescence. All of the girls accused of sex offenses are near the upper age limit.

Ninety per cent of the offenses of the native white boys are crimes against property. Of these one-third of the charges are for stealing or attempting to steal automobiles, this offense occurring more often than any other except "larceny," which includes all other stealing. With the exception of the stealing of automobiles the other white boys of English-speaking parentage (those from Canada, England, Scotland, and Ireland) so nearly resemble the sons of native white parents in the distribution of their offenses that they have been grouped together.

Contrasted with the English-speaking white children are the colored children. Only 50 per cent of their offenses were offenses against property, with only two instances of unlawful use of automobiles. The remaining 50 per cent of charges against colored children are 23 per cent offenses against person and 27 per cent runaway and stubborn complaints. These figures bear out the popular conception of the Negro as impetuous, sensual, wandering and philandering but not "vicious."

The North and South Europeans are quite similar in regard to type of offense. They stand about halfway between the native-white and colored in percentage of offenses against property (78 per cent of North Europeans, 73 per cent of South Europeans). Eleven per cent of North Europeans and 6 per cent of South Europeans were convicted of petty misdemeanors as compared with 1 per cent of English-speaking whites and no colored. In almost every case the offender pleaded ignorance of the specific ordinance violated, showing that a language handicap may have been a contributing factor.

The largest numbers of runaways were found among the colored and South Europeans—peoples with relatively low standards in the home, indicating the probability that undesirable home conditions or lack of opportunity for development may have influenced the child in committing the so-called offense. Table V summarizes these data.

TABLE V

Percentage distribution of offenses of 400 boys according to race-nativity-language groupings

Race-Nativity-Language Group	Type of Offense				
	I	II	III	IV	Total
English-speaking whites............	87	3	9	1	100
Colored	50	23	27	0	100
North Europeans.................	78	7	4	11	100
South Europeans.................	73	9	12	6	100

A similar analysis of the 100 girls' records shows no significant relationship, all types of offense being distributed proportionately in all nativity groups.

PREVIOUS DELINQUENCY

For all purposes of analysis and treatment the particular offense which is recorded as the behavior bringing the delinquent into court is important only as it forms a part of his entire life history. Often a very minor act is used as an excuse to apprehend a young "crook" whose adroitness has prevented his apprehension. During the course of investigation other deeds, more serious in nature, often come to light. The history of previous delinquency is derived from three sources: (1) the records of the Massachusetts Probation Commission; (2) the child's own story as told to the psychiatrist and sometimes to the probation officer; (3) information gleaned from parents and other members of the family, companions, school authorities, neighbors, and police officers.

The first source reports that 23 per cent of the boys and 2 per cent of the girls have previously been on probation, and that an additional 12 per cent of the boys and an additional 3 per cent of the girls have been arraigned in court for delinquent behavior. In some of the latter cases, lack of uniformity in the records makes it difficult to determine what disposition was made of the case. Of the boys with previous probation records, 47 per cent were kept on probation less than six months and 40 per cent between six months and one year. Both the girls served three month probation terms for the same offense as at present, namely, peddling without a license. The ninety-three male recidivists have an average age of 14.27 years as compared with 12.87 years for the boys who have never before been on probation.

So far as could be discovered from the other two sources of information, 21 per cent of the boys and 31 per cent of the girls have no history of previous delinquency. In short, only one-fifth of the boys and one-third of the girls are really first offenders.

Table VI shows also the length of time the remaining 318 boys and 69 girls have been misbehaving before they were apprehended. Twenty-two per cent of the boys and 35 per cent

TABLE VI

Duration of delinquency of 500 juvenile delinquents

Delinquent history	Boys		Girls	
	Number	Per cent	Number	Per cent
No previous delinquency............	82	21	31	31
Less than one year.................	88	22	35	35
One year to five years..............	182	45	27	27
Over five years....................	48	12	7	7
Total	400	100	100	100

of the girls had been experimenting with delinquency for less than one year.

Contrasted with these new recruits in crime are the 48 per cent of boys and 34 per cent of girls whose delinquent experience ranged from one to ten years.

Certain types of juvenile delinquency cause public consternation and are immediately dealt with. Fire-setting, ringing false alarms, larceny of automobiles, assault and battery, and forgery seldom pass unpunished. Many other offenses that are more demoralizing to the individual are not detected, or if detected, are allowed to go unchecked. Petty stealing and sex misconduct often continue for years without being discovered by parents. These two types of misbehavior comprise the majority of cases lasting more than five years listed in Table VI. Parents hope that their children will outgrow such undesirable traits as lying, sulking, stubbornness, disobedience, and selfishness and ignore them or deny their existence rather than admit to outsiders their own inadequacy to cope with the problem. Only where economic factors are involved (as when the child refuses to work or to surrender his pay envelope) or when the chastity of a daughter is endangered, will they appeal to the court. Offenses against property and wayward and stubborn behavior are the least likely to bring the child to court immediately.

MOTIVATIONS UNDERLYING DELINQUENCY

If not delinquency but the cause of delinquency is the important point for consideration, the imperative question becomes, not "What does Mary steal?" but "Why does Mary steal?"; not "What is the offense?" but "What needs or desires is the offender seeking to satisfy?" Many hypotheses have been tried out and discarded. Ideas surviving from antiquity that account for crime by "innate wickedness," "the possession of devils," and "natural cussedness" have been discarded. Theories of "criminal inheritance" and "biological transmission of moral imbecility" have been exploded. More recently "lack of recreational facilities," "bad neighborhood," and "feeble-mindedness" as blanket explanations have been repudiated by experts. Assertions that juvenile delinquency is due to "general lawlessness of youth" or the "crime wave" (which according to the press sweeps over the land engulfing the youth in much the same manner as a tidal wave inundates the land) are not only futile but are confusing.

Some sociologists are prone to interpret delinquency in terms of environmental factors,[7] while other sociologists as well as psychologists, psychiatrists, and social workers search for the motivation of behavior in the fundamental needs and desires of the child. The writings of Flügel, Taft, and Thomas, as well as the clinical studies of Healy, give illustrations of this point of view.[8]

Dr. Bernard Glueck, who for many years has worked with criminals, summarizes his conception of crime motivation thus:

"Increasing experience with these cases is gradually leading to a modification of our notions of predispositions and predestinations of one sort or another. We are less and less willing to attribute these manifestations to causes which are beyond the individual's experience, and incidentally beyond the reach of modification on

---

[7] Shaw, Clifford R., *Delinquency Areas;* and Sullenger, T. E., *Determinants in Juvenile Delinquency.*

[8] Flügel, J. C., *Psychoanalytic Study of the Family;* Taft, Jessie, "The Effects of an Unsatisfactory Mother-Daughter Relationship upon the Development of a Personality," *The Family,* 1926, Vol. 7, pp. 11-17; Thomas, W. I., *The Unadjusted Girl;* Healy, William, *The Individual Delinquent.*

this account. The tendency is increasingly in the direction of searching for the meaning of the disorder as part and parcel of a child's personality. What does the disorder or maladjustment signify as regards the personal economy of the child, as regards his life and functions as a feeling and striving and acting personality?

"When a boy steals or runs away from home or school, or is given to explosive tantrums of disobedience and rebellion, or is intimidated by the ordinary demands of daily life, what does it all mean? Do we satisfy the requirements of proper understanding when we call the boy a thief, or truant, or neurotic, or cowardly?

"Behind these outwardly simple categories of conduct with which we are so familiar and for the management of which law and custom have laid down certain fixed processes, there often lurks a complexity of phenomena which cannot be cleared up until we also ask ourselves, What is this boy after, what is he trying to achieve by these manifestations of conduct?

"Whether one is dealing with the mere tantrums of childhood, or with the more socially significant delinquency manifestations of stealing, lying or running away, it is essential above all to search for the meaning of the disorder in the child's economy, for the rôle it plays in the child's efforts to adapt himself to the demands of his environment. Frequently what the adult considers as an unhealthy or perverse manifestation of childhood behavior may be nothing less than the child's reactions to an imperative instinctive demand which must gain expression somehow, and it becomes our task not to thwart this energy expression by blind restriction, but to guide it into healthy channels of activity. More so even than the adult, the child in manifesting signs of maladjustment is merely attempting to reach some adjustment to a personality problem. His natural craving for recognition and for the enlargement of his personality renders him subject to all sorts of utilizations of his energies sometimes in a healthy normal manner, at other times in quite an abnormal fashion, in the service of his ego." [9]

"PROBABLE CAUSATIONS" LISTED BY THE JUDGE BAKER FOUNDATION

When the 500 children were being analyzed by the Clinic, many of the theories regarding motivation that are today

[9] Glueck, Bernard, "The Significance of Mental Hygiene in Child Guidance," *The Annals of the American Academy*, Vol. 121, p. 57.

TABLE VII

Causative factors in juvenile delinquency

	Number		
	Boys	Girls	Total
ENVIRONMENTAL			
Recreation	133	18	151
Bad Companion............................	207	51	258
Companionship Affair......................	105	12	117
Lack of Parental Control...................	176	50	226
Poverty	14	8	22
Poor Neighborhood	50	7	57
Opportunity	28	9	37
Victim....................................	4	1	5
Poor Work Adjustment.....................	12	0	12
Poor School Adjustment...................	4	0	4
Total Environmental......................	733	156	889
PERSONAL			
Mentality			
Supernormal	2	4	6
Defective..............................	49	20	69
Abnormal Personality...................	6	3	9
Personality Traits.........................	95	24	119
Ideation and Imagery.....................	170	52	222
Habits and Experience.....................	93	32	125
Circumstances	6	7	13
Physical Make-up.........................	28	7	35
Total Personal	449	149	598
Total	1182	305	1487

widely accepted, were then unformed, or at least unstated. Consequently the list of "causations" recorded would probably be redefined in more specific terms were they done at this time. Formerly no attempt was made by the Clinic to distinguish between what was subjective and what was objective. A factor listed as a primary cause might now be considered the ninety-ninth rung in the ladder rather than the first. Some items then called "causations" would today be termed "symptoms." Some statements are general, others are specific. For example, one record contains the expression "poor home situation," while another with similar conditions will list "alcoholism of father," "insufficient income," "quarreling of parents," "lack of harmony among children," and "parental cruelty and neglect."

However, the purpose of this particular part of the record was to bring to attention factors in the personality make-up and in the environment which seemed to be "determinants" in the child's delinquency. The probation officer usually based his work upon the Clinic's interpretation of these determinants.

That this method of presenting "causations" was efficacious is attested by both parents and probation officers. Hence it has seemed advisable to treat them as described. Even though this were not true, a study trying to evaluate the entire process of treatment could not ignore prevalent conceptions of causations.

More than sixty different items appear on the 500 schedules as having in some way contributed to the delinquency of these children. These items have been grouped and classified by the writer under the two headings "Environmental" and "Personal" as shown in Table VII. An effort is made to distinguish between misbehavior that is precipitated by external or objective elements and offenses that arise out of the internal or subjective conditions. The distinction is not clear-cut, but is suggestive of a line of study that might well be pursued further.

PROGNOSIS

To what avail is all this study of the delinquent's background, his mental capacity, the motivation of his behavior, and his history of misconduct? Does knowing the criminal career of a girl's grandfather, the attitudes of her mother toward marriage and childbearing, her age at teething, reactions toward her first playmates, her speed at arithmetical calculation, the frequency and subjects of her dreams, and the type of movies which she enjoys most, enable one to predict whether or not she will stop stealing, or to determine whether probation is preferable to foster home placement? Unfortunately none of these factors in themselves are of value in making predictions; but certain combinations of factors seem to occur with sufficient frequency in delinquent careers to warrant observation of them.

No objective scales have been devised that can tell what items in the social background of a specific individual are of greatest importance; there are no scales that can rate accurately either the "plus values" of personality or the "danger signals." Since no two individuals present the same combination of factors of personality and environment, the use of a scale would seem futile. Yet the expert through long experience is able to sense standards and rankings which assist him in making predictions. Child guidance clinics through their careful analysis of symptomatic behavior are thus able after a thorough study to give estimates of what will happen under given conditions.

When the Clinic findings are summarized, predictions are usually made regarding the chances of success and failure under specified conditions, and estimates are made of the possibilities of the child's continuing its delinquency. In the process of analyzing the 500 records, these predictions were arranged in order beginning with the most hopeful. No artificial classification was imposed; but the statements fell naturally into five grades suggesting to the writer the headings by which they are designated, namely, good, fair, poor, conditional, and deferred, or no prognosis. The quotations from records given below indicate the approximate meanings of the terms used.

Good. Prognosis may be termed good when there are no obvious factors to endanger the situation. Allowing for the beneficial effects of probation, the child is not likely to repeat its delinquency, for example:

> "Very likely not further delinquent."
> "Boy seems good sort, has pleasing personality and good interests."
> "No reason why girl should continue to be a behavior problem."
> "Distinctly good prognosis under present conditions."

Fair. A situation may be described as fair when it contains both desirable and undesirable elements, when there is a balance of helpful and dangerous factors, either within the make-up of the child or in his environment. To illustrate:

> "With proper management could well get satisfaction in other ways than delinquency."
> "Boy may settle down after this, but his father will probably be a disturbing factor."
> "Difficult situation, but mother takes a good attitude—may work out all right."

Poor. Poor prognosis implies that the dangers in the environment are so great or that the personality of the child is so distorted that the job of adjustment seems beyond the control of the probation officer, or of existing agencies.

> "Impossibly bad under old conditions."
> "No hopes for better behavior as things are going."
> "Likely to get into a good deal of trouble."
> "Material of which criminals are made."

Conditional. Sometimes two prognoses are given, one for one set of conditions and another for other conditions.

> "If this boy continues with this group, he is very likely to get into more serious trouble, but if the family moves as the father suggests, the outlook should be thoroughly good."
> "Will probably not be seriously delinquent if there is immediate attention given to physical needs, but if these are neglected, we see no chance for good adjustment."

Deferred. Often prognosis cannot be made in cases where the social investigation is found to be inadequate, where the child or parents did not coöperate in the clinical examination, or where the child needs further observation under controlled conditions, thus:

"Prognosis cannot be made without further information regarding the family situation."
"Unable to judge the present affair without seeing the girl's companions."

The percentage distributions of boys and girls receiving each type of prognosis are not dissimilar, as shown by the following list:

	Percentages	
	Boys	Girls
Good	42	48
Fair.........................	25	23
Poor	24	17
Conditional	4	6
Deferred.....................	4	6
None	1	0
Total	100	100

The Clinic does not feel that every juvenile delinquent is a "potential criminal." It believes that no further misdemeanors will be committed by one-half the children placed on probation. For about one-fourth of the boys and one-fifth of the girls, it does, however, issue warnings. It is saying to society: "Here is a situation fraught with danger. Unless something drastic is done, anti-social behavior is likely to result. The child with his present habits and attitudes and existing circumstances cannot be expected to refrain from further misconduct." The challenge is urgent.

RECOMMENDATIONS

A final criterion for estimating the problems of 500 juvenile delinquents is a summary of the Judge Baker Foundation recommendations. Attention is called to the nature of these recommendations. They are issued either as suggestions for trial, as, "It might be wise to be less rigid about Allen's bed time," or stated as commands, as, "Sarah must not be allowed to spend another night in her home under existing conditions." Some recommendations require months for their accomplishment, others only a few hours. Several different proposals, such as tutoring, providing satisfying recreation at school, or securing the teacher's interest in the child, might be directed toward the solution of one problem, truancy. On the other hand, the recommendation, "Send the boy to camp for two weeks," might cause the parents to realize the gravity of the child's misbehavior, introduce the boy to a new type of companion, or merely give him needed fresh air. But in every instance the suggestions represent the consensus of expert opinion. Every recommendation is based on scientific principles that have been handed down from criminology, psychiatry, and case work. The tentative programs appearing here represent decisions thoughtfully reached after consideration of both the immediate needs of the individual and his future outcome. Any unfulfilled need is a problem situation. But the prescribed treatment is not always concerned with the problem presented. "Help the boy get a job immediately" may be designed to enable a boy to earn some needed money or it may be a means of keeping a boy, who already has too much money, so occupied that he cannot spend his money in undesirable ways. The sum total of all recommendations is a fair guide to types of problem situations. From the mass of unanalyzed recommendations the following classification emerges:

Recommendations regarding:	Number of recommendations		
	Boys	Girls	Total
Home Life of the Delinquent....	294	88	382
Physical and Mental Life........	324	80	404
Companionship................	207	31	238
Recreation	163	34	197
Work	75	25	100
Education	114	34	148
Miscellaneous.................	72	20	92
Total Recommendations......	1249	312	1561

Health problems, while by no means the most important as far as delinquency is concerned, loom largest. One reason for the large number of recommendations for physical health lies in the more exact criteria for measurement of deviations in that field. The home situation of four-fifths of the children is likewise found to need modification. These recommendations call for change both in the physical environment of the home and in family attitudes and relationships. Suggestions are made for the improvement of companionship or of recreational activities for more than one-half of all the children. The work and the education of the delinquent child require the attention of society. A small number of recommendations deal with legal matters of the payment of restitution and length of term.

OUTCOME

Hereafter in this study "success," "permanent success," "continued success," and "success-to-date" are used synonymously to describe those boys and girls who ceased their delinquency before or during probation and for whom no subsequent records of misconduct have been discovered either in the files of the Massachusetts Probation Association or by social investigation. The term "temporary success" is used to describe persons whose probation was terminated satisfactorily but who subsequently have been delinquent. By "failure" is meant the persistence of delinquency in spite of probation. This category includes delinquents who were transferred to higher courts, those who ran away and were placed in default, and those who were sent to jail, a house of correction, a state reformatory, or a state training school. The number in each class is shown by the following list:

	Boys	Girls
Success	172	76
Temporary Success	135	12
Failure	85	12
Undetermined	8	0
Total	400	100

CONCLUSIONS

We have now answered the four groups of questions propounded at the beginning of this chapter. "What was the make-up of the group of delinquents studied?" "What were the offenses?" "Why were they committed?" and "What programs of treatment can be offered under probation?" The probation officer is naturally interested to know what relation these factors have to success on probation.

The make-up of the group. Who is the delinquent? To reiterate briefly, the group of 500 children described in this book is constituted as follows: Four-fifths are boys; the average age of boys is thirteen years and of girls fourteen years; nine-tenths are native born but four-fifths of the parents were foreign born; one-third of all parents speak English; four-fifths of the delinquents are within the normal range of mentality; two-fifths come from broken homes and four-fifths from homes on a low economic level.

With the exception of sex these factors when related to outcome on probation show no significant difference of success and failure. Although, as we shall see presently, the type of treatment must be suited to the individual child whether a genius or a moron, whether a recent immigrant or a five generation American, still these factors themselves do not preclude success or failure.[10]

The offenses. Approximately three-fourths of the group were guilty of stealing or other offenses against property. One-eighth of the children were brought to court on runaway or stubborn complaints, a larger proportion of girls than boys falling in this group. The remaining one-eighth is equally divided between sex offenses and petty misdemeanors. The only significant difference in outcome as related to offense is that among children committing offenses against property, who show a relatively larger degree of success than the other types of offenders.

More important than type of offense is the length of time

[10] See Appendix E, Tables, Nos. XX-XXXIII.

the offender has been engaged in delinquency. Two-fifths of the boys had a previous delinquent history of less than one year as compared with two-thirds of the girls. Although the average age of the girls was greater than that of the boys, a much larger number of boys had delinquent histories from one to five years and almost twice as many had continued their offenses for more than five years. Of all the pre-probation factors discussed in this chapter, duration of delinquency is more closely related to success and failure than any other factor.

Of the boy first offenders 64 per cent were successes as contrasted with 7 per cent failures. Among the girls 81 per cent of first offenders were successes while 3 per cent were failures. As duration of delinquency increases, the chances for permanent success decrease. The boy or girl who has been engaging in delinquency for more than a year has only one-half the chances of permanent success as has the first offender. The significance of this conclusion cannot be over-emphasized as it verifies what is shown repeatedly in this study, namely, that it is very important for the delinquent to be checked in his misconduct as soon as it becomes known.

Reasons for committing offenses. The explanations for anti-social behavior are so numerous and so complex that there is no short cut to their diagnosis. More than sixty different motivating factors and contributing causes in an infinite variety of combinations are listed for this group of 500 cases.

These causes, totaling more than fifteen hundred, may be classified as environmental and personal. Of the first type, bad companionship, lack of parental control, and poor recreations are cited most frequently for both boys and girls. Of the personal elements, mental conflict and undesirable ideation, personality deviations, and anti-social habits appear most often.

The relation of these causative factors to outcome is very definitely dependent upon social treatment; hence it is difficult to evaluate them. However, Tables XXVIII and XXIX in Appendix E indicate a greater degree of success for those persons whose delinquency is associated with companionship than for those whose delinquency is attributed to lack of parental control. The chapters, "Probation and Home Conditions" and "Probation and Companionship" suggest explanations for the differences.

Many correlations of outcome with probable causes of delinquency, both individually and in combination, were calculated, but due to the complexity and overlapping of the "causations" none of the coefficients were large enough to be considered significant. They prove significant only when related to each other, to the type and duration of the offense, and to the specific treatment given. These will be discussed in detail in subsequent chapters.

Programs for treatment. The Clinic study includes not only a description of the individual, his offenses, and reasons for committing them, but also gives a prognosis for his success and a program for his treatment.

For almost one-half of the group the Clinic predicted success on probation, while for one-fourth the prognosis was decidedly unfavorable. Of the boys given good prognoses by the Clinic, only 9 per cent were failures, while of the boys given poor prognoses, only 25 per cent were successes. Where a good prognosis was made for the girls, 92 per cent were successes, where the prognosis was poor, 53 per cent were failures.

The expert study of the delinquent proved especially valuable. Coefficients of contingency were calculated between all the factors outlined in this chapter and outcome.[11] Of these, *the Clinic prognosis was the only coefficient large enough to be considered significant.*

The recommendations made by the Clinic fall into six groups: namely, home conditions, physical and mental life, companionship, recreation, work, and education. A chapter is devoted to a detailed discussion of each of these topics. It must always be remembered that whereas the suggestions are stated in terms of concrete situations, they often involve sud-

[11] The class in Social Statistics at Bryn Mawr College, working under the direction of Professor Susan M. Kingsbury and Miss Jeanette Gruener, Research Assistant in the Department of Social Economy and Social Research, assisted the writer in computing coefficients of contingency to measure the relationships between outcome on probation and thirty-seven pre-probation factors and types of probation treatment. Miss Ona Meigs Fowler also assisted in these and other statistical computations.

den changes of attitudes, personal relationships, and emotional states. It is only in relation to specific recommendations and the extent to which they were carried out that the outcome can be determined.

In the succeeding chapters the aim is to show how probation as a form of social treatment may be used to solve the problems of the delinquent child. Each of the six phases of his life situation is discussed in relation to the problem as presented, the probation officer's method of treatment, and success and failure on probation.

CHAPTER III

PROBATION AND THE HOME LIFE OF THE DELINQUENT

The first requisite of wholesome childhood is an environment promoting physical and social development. The home is the institution that normally fulfils this function. Society at the present time accords to parents the privilege and the responsibility of the care and guidance of the children. Only when the home situation presents very grave dangers does society interfere to remove the child or to attempt other adjustment.

The 500 boys and girls who are studied here as probation cases were not all left in the home because it was considered the ideal environment for them. Indeed, conditions of many were atrociously bad. The Clinic, in more than one-fourth of the cases, had pronounced the home environment inadequate or menacing and had urged that the child be removed. For a few others it recommended transfer to institutions for the feeble-minded, and industrial schools for boys and girls needing severe disciplinary training. In these cases two purposes are evident: first, to provide the training commensurate with the child's ability and needs; and second, to protect society from the depredations of the child. That the recommendations of the Clinic were not followed does not indicate lack of agreement on the part of the Court. Some children were placed on probation because their parents would not permit them to be sent to institutions or to be placed in foster homes; some, because other facilities were lacking.

In order to bring about an improvement in environmental conditions, the probation officer uses three types of treatment: (1) removal of the child, where the home is hopelessly inadequate; (2) transplanting the home into another neighborhood, where the influence of the family itself is good, but not strong enough to counteract the bad influences of the neighborhood; (3) case work on the family, where the physical surroundings of the home and neighborhood are adequate but where personal relationships are not conducive to harmony and happiness.

The remainder of this chapter is devoted to an analysis of these three types of treatment, giving for each: first, the extent of the problem; second, the work of the probation officer in remedying the situations; and third, the outcome.

REMOVAL OF THE CHILD FROM THE HOME

Children may be removed from their homes and sent to other homes or to institutions. The following table summarizes the recommendations made by the Judge Baker Foundation for the temporary or permanent care of children in different environments.

	Boys	Girls	Total
Send to institution for the feeble-minded....	13	2	15
Commit to state training schools..........	8	3	11
Place in foster homes or with relatives......	89	21	110
Enroll in boarding school................	5	1	6
Secure work and board away from home....	8	2	10
Remove from home temporarily, for special study or treatment, or to go to caddy camp, seashore or the country for vacation.................................	55	0	55
Total	178	29	207

The Clinic recommended commitment of fifteen children to institutions for the feeble-minded. The results of the probation officer's work with these fifteen children is most encouraging. Three children had to be sent later to institutions for the feeble-minded for they not only persisted in misbehavior themselves but were considered a menace to their neighborhoods; and one boy was sent to a state training school, one defaulted and has never been located, and one was transferred to a higher court. But the remaining cases were satisfactorily dealt with on probation, and only two of the nine were found by this study to have been guilty of additional delinquencies. Adjustment in these cases was due to change to a special school or special class for backward children, moving away from bad companions, employment (usually at routine work) under good supervision, or "case work on the family" resulting in greater understanding of the limitations of the children.

Every one of the eleven delinquents for whom disciplinary institutions were recommended continued misbehavior regardless of the efforts of the probation officers. The Court finds it necessary to remove from society children whose long continued habits of delinquency make them a menace to others. It is not that the probation officer could not solve their problems. They might be as efficacious as the directors of training schools, but the Court cannot run the risk of the child's continued depredations during the long process of developing substitutive habits. Hence the child is removed from society until his attitudes and habits can be changed. With only one exception all eleven proved to be unmanageable and had to be committed sooner or later.

The term of foster home care does not necessarily coincide with the term of probation, although it is a usual practice for the Court to continue supervision until the child has been returned to his home and has shown his ability to readjust to that environment. It often happens, however, that in the case of long continued care, especially where there are abnormal mental or personality characteristics, the Court files the case, leaving care entirely to the agency. It is not the purpose of this study to describe the work of child placing agencies or the results of their treatment, since this topic has been treated very thoroughly by Dr. Healy and his associates.[1] The cases are cited here only to show the extent to which the two types of treatment overlap and the use that the probation officer makes of "placing." During the course of their proba-

[1] Healy, Bronner, Baylor and Murphy, *Reconstructing Behavior in Youth.*

tion sixty-two boys and fourteen girls were sent to foster homes. The terms ranged in length from a few weeks to five years, five boys being still under the care of the agencies. In one-half of the cases the probation officers enlisted the efforts of child placing agencies; for the others, the officers themselves found the foster homes and visited the children. No significant difference in outcome is seen between the young people who were placed and those who were not. However it is safe to assume that the difference would have been great for the two groups if the former had not been placed, as in most cases they were handicapped by poor home influences or bad companions or both. A distinction must be made between this long-time separation of children from parents and temporary placement. Seventy-one boys and girls were temporarily removed from their homes in order to facilitate physical upbuilding or recuperation, to secure work, to provide education of a specific type, to separate them from bad companions, or to acquire new habits or attitudes. More detailed discussion of these cases will be presented in subsequent chapters dealing with each of these topics.

One justification of punishment is that by temporarily isolating the offender, he may come to realize that he wants and needs social status, and that happiness lies in social conformity. At the very earliest possible moment, then, opportunity should be given the offender to experience pleasure from coöperation. A feeling of contrition is expressed by the statements: "I have behaved badly"; "I have committed a wrong"; "I am looked down upon by society because I have taken what did not belong to me"; "I have embarrassed my family by causing them to be summoned to court." "I am so ashamed of my behavior that I do not wish to face my teacher." These statements may have value in as much as they represent a step in the orientation of the individual and are prerequisite to an integration of personality. However, it cannot be stressed too often that these negative attitudes and feelings have no value for society. No constructive work has been done with the individual until he has progressed beyond this stage. The delinquent must see how more pleasure can be obtained by fitting into a constructive social pattern. This cannot be accomplished until opportunity is given for constructive activities. It is not being sorry for having done wrong or being willing to conform to social standards that makes a useful citizen; it is doing the things that characterize the good citizen. For this reason probation has many advantages over institutional care of delinquents. Where the home is adequate, it is seldom necessary to separate the child from the home for any length of time in order to make him realize his loss in the separation. Opportunities for useful activity should follow immediately upon resolve.

TRANSPLANTING THE HOME

A form of social treatment slightly, if any, less drastic than that of removing the child from the home, is that of transplanting the whole family to a new neighborhood. To determine the value of so rigorous treatment, this study attempts to answer the following questions: (1) Under what conditions, or for what reasons would a probation officer deem it his prerogative to dictate where a family should or should not live? (2) What methods does the probation officer use in order to change the habitat of a family? (3) To what extent is the probation officer able to make the desired adjustment? (4) Does moving a child away from the scene of his delinquency stop the delinquency, or prevent its recurrence?

To hear that an officer of the law said to one out of every five families "You must move" suggests the plagues of Jehovah visited upon the Egyptians. This condition, one would think, would be found in a despotic and not in a democratic country. Yet that is exactly what happened to the families of ninety-seven juvenile delinquents. Either the Clinic or the Court suggested that they should move away from the neighborhoods in which they were living when their children committed the offenses. For forty-eight boys and eight girls this recommendation was made at the time of examination; for twenty-seven boys and fourteen girls moving was advised because in 90 per cent of the cases the requirement that the child be taken away could not be carried out.

The chief reasons for transplanting families seem to have been: (1) to escape the degrading influences of "bad" neighborhoods; (2) to separate the child from bad companions and to put him in contact with children of a higher type; (3) to have access to better recreational facilities; (4) to escape from unhygienic and unsanitary living quarters and to provide fresh air and sunshine for persons needing physical upbuilding; (5) to attain a higher general plane of living and to give new impetus to both parents and children by the opportunity to "begin with a clean slate."

Although "bad neighborhood conditions" had not been formally defined by the Clinic, it was used in these records to describe neighborhoods where bootlegging, drinking, exhibitionism, accosting, or gambling were openly practised or where standards in general were low, permitting profanity, vulgarity, and violation of the law. In no instance was the neighborhood rated "bad" for purely sanitary or hygienic reasons, or because of the lack of proper housing requirements or recreational facilities. These factors have been listed separately in so far as they have any connection with delinquency; as, for example, in seven instances, where the family was urged to move to the country or suburbs in order that nervous and undeveloped children might have better opportunity for normal growth. That "bad" neighborhood was listed in only one-half the cases does not mean that the other half lived in desirable neighborhoods. The summary of "Probable Causations" (Chapter II, p. 31) shows that the delinquency of fifty boys and seven girls was attributed in part to the influences of the district.

How Can the Probation Officer Cause a Family to Move? In many cases foreign families were living in the crowded immigrant districts to which they had been led when they first arrived. At that time their lack of English, inability to pay higher rents, and desire to be near their countrymen prevented their settling in outlying regions. Although these factors were no longer operative, mere apathy or ignorance of better localities detained them. Many parents expressed dissatisfaction with their surroundings and gave the probation officer or the Clinic social worker opportunity to suggest moving by their remarks, as for example: "I can never keep Tony out of mischief when every time he steps outside his own door he sees wrong doing," or "My girl is herself not low down, but she sees other people doing what's wrong and getting by with it and what I say don't count."

The effort involved in moving cannot be measured in physical activity alone. The records show that the task of making up one's mind to be separated from one's neighbors is not always easy, and the anticipation of contact with strange people is frequently not pleasurable. Hence, if some steps are not taken immediately and the child appears to be all right, parents are likely to slump and remain where they are.

The probation officers worked persistently and ingeniously to carry out these recommendations. Not only did they suggest more desirable districts, but they made contacts for parents with real estate dealers and landlords. In some cases the probation officer when going to visit a suburban area invited prospective "movers" to accompany him in order that they might see the difference in living conditions.

Occasionally the officer threatened to remove the child if the family did not yield, and in eight instances the Clinic recommended, "Send the child to live with relatives or friends until the family moves."

The question might be asked, "Why not clean up the neighborhood for the protection of all the children rather than remove the ones who are already contaminated?" This study records many instances of efforts to change neighborhood conditions. City lights were placed in dark alleys where gangs had met unobserved in the semi-darkness. Extra policemen were placed in districts where violation of the law was reported. The two vicious sex-perverts who were responsible for the practices of eighteen boys included in this study were sentenced to prison. "Speakeasies" and gambling dens were closed. Men and women trafficking in stolen goods were apprehended.

But the improvement of a neighborhood of ill repute is a slow process and cannot be depended upon for immediate remedial effect.

Does Moving the Family Reform the Child? As a result of their contact with the Clinic and Court one out of every eight families improved its physical environment by moving. Of course, many other families during this period took other apartments within the same tenement or in other tenements within the same district. Some of these changes improved slightly the situation of the family, but as a rule they were made without relation to the Court's wishes or advice.

In 60 per cent of the sixty-eight families who moved, probation for the child was counted a success. In another 13 per cent, delinquency ceased for a while; and in only 16 per cent of the whole group the change of districts did not affect the behavior of the child. Salvatore F. is a typical example of the beneficial effects of living in a new neighborhood.

Salvatore had been allowed considerable free time on the street because his mother had four small children who "made enough noise without having Salvatore around to tease them." Both Mr. and Mrs. F. had been indignant over complaints made by merchants of the neighborhood that Salvatore and his gang had broken in and stolen food, toys, and clothing. Mr. F. had beaten Salvatore unmercifully when upon two occasions he had had to pay restitution to the merchants; but these problems had always been settled without recourse to the law. Recently Salvatore had been truanting from school, staying out late at night, and neighbors had warned Mrs. F. that he was smoking and drinking. When Salvatore was arrested with his gang for breaking into a radio factory, his parents felt that their son had "gone to the devil," and wanted him sent away. The parents were made to see that Salvatore's delinquencies were not a result of any desire on his part to be wicked, but were his attempts to find some exciting way of passing the time. When the family moved to a suburban home where there was a swimming pool near by and a playground for baseball and other sports, Salvatore was just as easily attracted to athletics as he had been to "crooking." The boys with whom he played ball did not truant, so Salvatore was never found guilty of this offense. Although Mr. F.

found the long ride to his work unpleasant at first, he soon appreciated the peace and quiet of his new home. Mrs. F. was shocked into realizing that her duty to her children included provision for their recreation, so urged Salvatore to bring his new friends to his home in the evening.

Age seems to be the most important factor in determining the effectiveness of moving. When children are under thirteen, moving is a satisfactory means of breaking up undesirable companionships; but when they are over thirteen, it accomplishes this result in only one case in four. Obviously, moving cannot solve problems arising within the family relationship.

Where recommendations for moving were not followed, more than one-half of the children either continued their delinquency or repeated it within a few months after probation ended.

Dan B. had a long history of petty delinquency and more recently had been stealing money from home. There had been no effort at deterrence. Dan was considered by the Clinic "a bright boy, thoroughly reformable," but it advised, "Family must move away from this neighborhood, not only to separate the boy from his bad companions with whom he has been associated in all his mischief, but also because of the father's previous bad record, which causes the boy some embarrassment here." The parents promised to move away from Boston in the spring. In the meantime, Dan joined a settlement house club at the request of the probation officer, and had his teeth filled at a dental clinic. He stopped bringing to his home the bad companions with whom he was told not to associate. He reported to the Court regularly, saying that all was going well with him. About four months later the father came to Court to say that Dan had run away a week ago, and had not been heard of since. When located, he was taken back to the Clinic for further study and the following report was made: "This boy has been doing decidedly poorly. Nothing that we recommended has been done. The family has not moved. His bad companionship has been kept up. At present he is going with a group of especially bad boys. Seems thoroughly weak, vacillating, somewhat of a coward, long in the habit of taking the easiest course. Not sensitive in general, but seems loyal to his family. Prognosis is thoroughly poor under the present conditions. Chances of his making good, with his established associations of companionship in that neighborhood, are very slim indeed. If family cannot move, boy must be placed either with relatives or in a foster home, or sent to some institution such as the Good Will Farm in Maine, or the Connecticut George Jr." Again a period of several months elapsed, during which time the probation officer made frequent visits to the home, and discussed various plans with the boy and his parents; but no decisive steps were taken. Dan ran away again, was caught in an automobile his friends had stolen, and was sent to one of the state training schools.

The relation between the incidence of crime and urban ecology has been clearly demonstrated by other writers.[2] Undoubtedly more careful city planning would itself decrease the proportion of juvenile crime. But as successful as moving was in the cases studied, this form of treatment has obvious limitations. If all the families left "bad neighborhoods," they would probably form aggregations in other localities that would soon show signs of deterioration. In other words, changing locality can at best only result in changes of habits.

CASE WORK ON THE FAMILY

One might think, to read the list of factors contributing to juvenile delinquency (Chapter II, p. 31) that the parents of the children studied had memorized Dr. Miriam Van Waters' "nineteen ways of being a bad parent" and had tried them all.[3] Lack of parental control was considered responsible for the delinquency of almost one-half of the children (176 boys and 50 girls). Schoolteachers, club leaders and social workers are often heard to say, "It is not the child but his parents who need treatment." What can the probation officer do to reform ignorant, lazy, immoral, cruel, selfish, or thoughtless parents? Can parents be put on probation?

No step in the treatment of juvenile delinquency is taken

[2] Shaw, Clifford R., *Delinquency Areas;* Shaw, Clifford R., "Correlation of Juvenile Delinquency with Community Organization and Disorganization," *Proceedings of American Sociological Society,* Vol. XXII, pp. 174-179; Sullenger, T. Earl, *Social Determinants in Juvenile Delinquency;* Zorbaugh, Harvey W., *Gold Coast and Slum.*
[3] Van Waters, Miriam, *Parents on Probation,* Chapter IV.

with the child alone. When a child is summoned to court, his parents are summoned to bring him. The judge questions and advises both parents and child. The Clinic interviews both father and mother, if possible, and discusses with them the life situation of the child, his relations to them, and their responsibilities toward him. Well-meaning, but busy or harassed parents welcome suggestions from persons who "understand" their children. Ignorant and unconcerned parents have to be educated. But at all times treatment of the child's problems is planned with the parents and, if the probation officer is very skillful, is developed by the parents, working, of course, upon ideas that have been subtly imparted by the officer. "Secure the coöperation of parents" is as necessarily a fundamental dictum as "Win the confidence of the child."

While almost all case work presupposes the coöperation of parents, the Clinic found it necessary in almost one-fourth of the cases to make specific suggestions for treatment of parents or home conditions. These recommendations fall into two classes, first, those relating to attitudes; and second, those relating to habits or practices.

The following outline, drawn from the records of the Foundation, presents suggestions for probation practice. It will perhaps be of most value if presented in this form, followed by illustrations of the way in which the instructions have been carried out.

JUDGE BAKER FOUNDATION RECOMMENDATIONS REGARDING CASE
WORK ON THE FAMILY

I. Change of Attitude
    1. Influence the parents and siblings to sympathize with the interests of the child.
    2. Persuade the parents to be less severe.
        a. Recognize physical and mental limitations.
        b. Stop cruelty.
        c. Stop scoldings and recriminations.
        d. Allow privileges (to keep animals, to join clubs).
    3. Convince the parents that they must give more attention to the needs of the child.

    a. Face parental responsibility.

    b. Give better supervision.

    c. Realize seriousness of the child's delinquency.

    d. Be less shielding.

    e. Allow less spending money.

4. Clarify family misunderstandings by careful explanation.

    a. Resolve conflict regarding adopted parents, foster parents, and deserted parents.

5. Give parents intelligent attitude toward sex habits and the steps to take in helping the child to overcome them.

6. Explain to parents the need for serious operations or commitment to institution for the feeble-minded.

II. Create Proper Home Environment

1. Correct menacing conditions in members of the household.

    a. Check the behavior of parents and siblings who are violating the law.

    b. Explain the necessity for attention to physical and mental needs of the other members of the family.

    c. Remove from the home boarders or relatives who exert a bad influence.

2. Build up the family morale by encouragement and praise.

3. Persuade the family to apply to a family case working agency, and secure the coöperation of the agency.

The parents of Caesar J. illustrate the conflicts of attitudes with which the probation officer must deal.

Mr. J. was a highly respected and fairly prosperous merchant in Genoa. He had reared a family of four fine sons, all of whom were holding responsible jobs in other cities in Italy. When his wife died, he was persuaded by friends to come to America. He got a good position in a wholesale fruit store. Being lonely, he married a young, vivacious Italian woman. Their one child, Caesar, was the source of constant disagreement. Mr. J. constantly held up as a standard the good behavior of his sons in Italy; he believed that Caesar should be beaten into conformity with his ideal. Mrs. J., on the other hand, demanded for her son the rights and privileges of American youth. Caesar soon learned that he could depend upon his mother to intercede and prevent his getting whippings from his stern father. He learned, too, that it was easy to escape punishment by skillful lying. When Caesar was arrested for breaking into a store at night, his father felt that this boy, so different from his other sons, had disgraced him, and demanded that the judge "put him away." The mother pleaded for Caesar and promised the judge that she would give better supervision. Clearly, Caesar was not an "institutional case," that is, his delinquencies were not so serious as to make him a menace to society; yet he could not be allowed to continue in his carefree way, feeling that "anything is all right if you can get by with it."

The task of the probation officer was to bring together the divergent views of the parents, so that one standard of behavior could be demanded, and the boy required to accept it as authority. In order to avoid for the boy the severe beatings which his father would be sure to inflict upon him, and in order to convince the mother that her too shielding attitude would eventually lead to the loss of her son, it was considered necessary to remove him from the home for a while. He was not committed to a training school, however, but was sent to live with an uncle who had a farm in an outlying district. The probation officer explained the situation to the uncle and asked him to give Caesar careful supervision, allowing privileges, but insisting that commands be enforced. The boy, by the separation from his home and from the protection of his mother, was made to realize that he must respect authority, and that he must have a sense of honor regarding his own actions. In the meantime, the probation officer had frequent interviews with the parents. He helped the father to see the life of the normal American boy as contrasted with the life of the Italian boy, and showed him how he was causing his wife and son to practise deception by making demands which to them were tyrannical. On the other hand, the probation officer showed the mother that she was undermining the boy's character by her unwarranted protection; and told her that her son could not return to her until she was willing to coöperate with the father and with the probation officer in a careful check-up on the boy's behavior.

The work of the probation officer in rehabilitating the home of Phyllis E. indicates another type of situation.

Phyllis was arrested in a department store for attempting to charge on the account of a neighbor a complete new outfit, spring coat, three dresses, two hats, shoes, and underwear. When they appeared in Court, both she and her mother presented a striking contrast to the shabbily clothed persons who filled the room. Mrs. E. was described thus: "Young woman of fine physique. Regular attractive features; simply dressed in sports outfit; refined appearance and manner. Expresses herself extremely well, in a pleasant, well-modulated voice. Assumes to perfection the rôle of a mother whose main interest in life is her children, and who has devoted herself to giving them the most wholesome upbringing possible."

In contrast to this picture the social history is rather sordid. Mr. E. was born in Italy of English parents. When in university, he got into trouble and was sent by his parents to America. He was described as "a sporty type, who drank like a gentleman." He owned and managed a riding academy, making a great deal of money. Mrs. E. spent much of her time at resorts and hotels, leaving her five children in the care of servants. The home was described as one of luxury. Two years previous to Phyllis' escapade, her father's health had broken, and he was placed in a private sanitorium. Mrs. E. tried to continue the business, but did not do well. She had as her chief helper the riding master who soon came to live with her. Neighbors reported that "crates of liquor were piled to the chandeliers," and that the "children were running wild." Phyllis had left home and was staying with some friends of her father in a suburb.

Knowing these facts, the probation officer discussed with Mrs. E. the necessity for living on a simple scale since the family income was greatly reduced. On the basis of the mother's concern over her children a plan was worked out in detail. The probation officer went with her to rent an apartment and stood by until the lease was signed. Then before Mrs. E. could change her mind or step out of her rôle, the officer introduced her to the president of the Parent-Teacher's Association in her neighborhood, and assured the latter of Mrs. E.'s interest and coöperation. She talked to the clergyman of the church with which Mrs. E. claimed affiliation and within a week Mrs. E. had been called upon by several ladies and was enrolled in a church club.

Whether it was Mrs. E.'s dramatic sense and the appreciation of the part she was playing, or whether it was her real interest in her children that brought the reformation cannot be known, but after five years Mrs. E. and her family are firmly implanted in the life of that neighborhood and all the children have good records to date. The break with her old life was not so decisive as the above paragraph would indicate, for Mrs. E. was known to have gone on several "business trips" to Atlantic City where she met the riding master, but these reversions became less and less frequent and were finally discontinued.

Much of the work of the probation officer is directed toward changing the attitude of parents toward their children and of children toward their parents. At least seven adopted children needed this kind of treatment. In four cases break-down of morale is attributed to conflict arising over the discovery that they are adopted. In the other three cases strange antipathies toward foster parents make any congenial home adjustment impossible. Attention will be called in subsequent chapters to the necessity for the probation officer to change parents' attitudes toward their children's schooling, work, recreation, and companions. This type of treatment seemed especially difficult for the probation officers.

The probation officer working with girls was more successful in carrying out the recommendation regarding home life than the ones working with boys. For girls, 65 per cent of the home problems were solved, but for boys, only 36 per cent. In the girls' cases, particularly, the fact was repeatedly made evident that it is as important that over-severe parents become more lenient as that lax parents become more severe. Often parents must be urged to use patience and sympathy.

Outcome in Relation to Case Work on the Family. Case work on the family is time well spent. In fifty-nine cases where the instructions were carried out, all children (that is, thirty-nine boys and twenty girls) were filed as successes. Only one boy whose family received the prescribed treatment had a subsequent court record. Where the treatment was attempted but not fulfilled (sixteen cases), the percentage of failure is four times that of success. In the remaining forty-six cases where no attempt at case work is recorded, the percentage of failure is equal to that of temporary success, and at last report more than three-fourths of the entire number were delinquent.

SUMMARY AND CONCLUSIONS

Under normal conditions the home is considered the ideal milieu for the child, but inadequate equipment or vicious influences in the home, or disease, or defect of the child may make separation from the home or neighborhood desirable. For children whose delinquency is attributed to poor environmental conditions, the Clinic proposes three solutions: (1) removal of the child from the home; (2) removal of the home from the neighborhood; (3) case work on the family.

Recommendations of foster home or institutional care were made for approximately one-fourth of the children. But all were placed on probation either because their parents were unwilling to have their children separated from them or because facilities for their care were lacking. During the course of their probation, however, officers placed in foster homes a total of seventy-six boys and girls. The majority were persons for whom placement was originally recommended; the others were children whose home situations changed during probation. Of the fifteen children for whom institutions for the feeble-minded were recommended, ten were successfully handled on probation. Morons may become useful citizens if attention is given to securing calm and happy family relationships, simple work, and protection from bad companions. Ten of the eleven children for whom state training schools were advised were eventually committed.

One out of every five families were urged by the Clinic or Court to move. In more than one-half of these cases "bad neighborhood conditions" had contributed to the child's delinquency. Many of the families were dissatisfied with their surroundings and needed only the encouragement of the probation officer to induce them to move. About three-fourths of the families who were advised to move, did so. Moving proved to be an effective way of breaking up bad companionship for younger children, but not for those over thirteen. The percentage of success at last report was more than twice as great for children in families who moved as in families who were urged to move but did not.

Treatment of the delinquent child must often be supplemented by treatment of the parents. The Clinic made definite recommendations for treatment of the parents of 122 children. These recommendations involved changes of parental attitudes and new habit formations. Where congenial family relationships are established, success on probation is almost certain. Where hates, jealousies, and misunderstandings of parents and children persist, the percentage of failure is four times that of success.

CHAPTER IV

PROBATION AND PHYSICAL AND MENTAL HEALTH

"Social Pathology" is the term used to include poverty, insanity, crime, unemployment, and many other so-called diseases of society. The connection between pathology and crime is neither remote nor figurative. Criminologists have for many years sought to discover relationships between distorted minds and malformed and malfunctioning bodies and the incidence of crime. Lombroso's theory of biological degeneracy finds a modern counterpart in Adler's theory that social maladjustment often results from "organ inferiority." [1]

This chapter attempts to determine for 500 juvenile delinquents first, the amount of physical inferiority, disease, and defect, and the relation between these handicaps and delinquency; and second, the relation between inner mental life and delinquency. The investigation of the first problem resolves itself into three questions: (1) What is the physical status of the children? (2) What can the probation officer do to correct physical handicaps? (3) How is improved physical condition related to improved conduct?

THE PHYSICAL CONDITION OF 500 JUVENILE DELINQUENTS

Three-fourths of all the children suffered from slight physical difficulties at the time of their examination or during the course of their probation. Only one-fourth (106 boys and 27 girls) were physically sound in that no defects had been noted. Inasmuch as few people of any social group are absolutely perfect physical specimens, it may well be that these cases

---

[1] Adler, Alfred, *The Theory and Practice of Individual Psychology*, Chapter 25, pp. 306-16.

do not differ greatly from non-delinquents coming from the same type of home. The physically imperfect may be divided into two groups: first, those who have major physical problems such as diseases of the heart, lungs, stomach or other vital organs; and second, those who present physical problems of less imminent danger, such as carious teeth, enlarged tonsils, slight astigmatism, and mild cases of malnutrition.

The first group includes 15 per cent of the boys and 24 per cent of the girls. For the majority of this group or for more than one-tenth of all the cases (fifty-three boys and eleven girls) the health recommendation was the most important one. The following statements are illustrative of these cases:

This boy needs most of all a chance to grow. His family must be made to provide wholesome food and to have his tonsils removed immediately.

Most of this girl's troubles can be traced to her poor physical condition. It is criminal that her parents have not allowed her to be examined before. Every effort must be made to build her up physically before any other treatment is attempted.

No other type of problem appears so frequently as those classified under "Health Problems." Furthermore, the estimate of "Health Problems" is based upon the number of persons for whom some recommendation was made and not upon the total number of specific recommendations. More than one-fifth of all Judge Baker Foundation recommendations are concerned with the health of the child. In terms of treatment each specific item represents a "problem." That is to say, for the 294 boys referred to, 555 needs were indicated (see Table VIII). And for the seventy-three girls needing medical attention, 152 items were mentioned. The persons who were not entirely sound and healthy presented an average of two conditions each needing treatment.

Almost one-half the children (181 boys and 45 girls) had carious teeth, one-third of them had enlarged or diseased tonsils. Defective vision, digestive disorders, venereal diseases, and nose and throat diseases or defects were each found in forty or more cases.

The defects and diseases listed here are the unrecognized or unheeded ailments of supposedly normal children. That they were not discovered and remedied earlier is due to the ignorance and neglect of parents and, to a lesser extent, to the carelessness and inefficiency of schoolteachers and others who have come in contact with them. Children suffering from anemia and other forms of malnutrition are scolded by their parents for laziness. Children hard of hearing are accused by parents and teachers of stupidity and of disobedience when they have not understood what was expected of them. Even advanced cases of tuberculosis, diseases of the heart and kidneys, and venereal diseases were not detected by parents.

PROBATION TREATMENT

The Clinic accomplishes the first step in health treatment. The physician, in his confidential conversation with the child, helps him to face his weakness squarely and to recognize his strength. He anticipates the objections to wearing glasses, or abstaining from strenuous exercise, or wearing braces on his ankles. He knows that the boy fears nothing so much as the ridicule of other boys. He dispels this fear by meeting it openly and saying, "Of course, the fellows will try to tease you at first; but you can always reply ———." Parents are particularly appreciative of the suggestions made by the Clinic: first, because they feel that the workers "understand" their children; and second, because the advice is given to them without charge and the treatment is to be carried on by someone else. They do not feel that the Clinic doctors have ulterior motives in their recommendations. The probation officer's task is to see that the prescribed treatment is obtained.

The sum total of medical ministrations leaves no doubt that the physical well being of 500 children has been markedly improved by their probation experience. More than one hundred had teeth treated or filled. More than one hundred had their tonsils or adenoids or both removed; and thirty others had operations or treatment for diseases or defects of ears, nose, or throat. Almost fifty children secured glasses or re-

TABLE VIII

Judge Baker Foundation recommendations for boys and girls

For treatment for defect or disease of:	Recommendations attempted		Recommendations Not attempted	Grand Total
	Fulfilled	Not fulfilled		
Teeth	97	13	116	226
Tonsils and adenoids	104	9	56	169
Eyes.....................	45	1	31	77
Digestive organs	22	4	19	45
Reproductive organs .... (venereal diseases, 10)	21	6	14	41
Nose and throat..........	16	2	22	40
Skin and scalp	11	1	11	23
Ears.....................	14	0	8	22
Endocrine glands	6	2	3	11
Heart	2	1	5	8
Posture	5	0	2	7
Respiratory organs	3	0	2	5
Cervical glands	2	0	2	4
Kidneys	2	0	2	4
Bones	1	1	1	3
Miscellaneous	12	5	5	22
Total	363	45	299	707

ceived treatment for diseases of the eye. In twenty-two cases children were given medicine or followed diet lists for the correction of poor digestion or metabolism. Almost as many persons (ten boys and eleven girls) were treated for venereal disease. Other types of malady involving a long period of care that was successfully followed through were endocrine disturbances, malfunctioning of the heart and kidneys, poor posture, and respiratory diseases. But of the total 707 demands for medical attention only one-half were met. The only recommendations that were fulfilled in more than one-half the cases were for glasses and for the removal of tonsils and adenoids. (See Table VIII on page 62.)

The amount of time and attention required of the probation officer for health work varies from one discussion lasting less than one-half hour to weekly exhortations extending over a period of months or even years. In one court record fifty-four references to medical attention appeared. The author estimated that the probation officer must have spent at least 200 hours in his efforts to convince the parents of one boy that he needed treatment and to enlist the coöperation of physicians and social workers.

The agencies most often used by the probation officer in carrying out health recommendations are: school nurses, social service departments of the city hospitals and of other clinics and hospitals, and private physicians. The latter are sometimes personal friends of the probation officer, who are persuaded to give their services without pay or for a minimum fee, and sometimes friends of the family, whose services are enlisted at the suggestion of the family. Of the two phases of the probation officer's task—securing the coöperation of the child and his family, and putting them in contact with facilities for treatment—it is difficult to say which requires more skill and persistence. When physicians are busy and clinic calendars are filled up for weeks in advance, unfortunately, it requires "pull," the ability to make dramatic appeals, and tactful and persistent effort to have "just one other" patient admitted. Here the reason that treatment must not be delayed does not always lie in the dangerous condition of the malady, but in the purpose to be served by securing the treatment.

Establishment of rapport with the family is much facilitated through consideration of health. No question is so natural and easy to ask as "How do you do?" "How are you feeling today?" No question is more conducive to parental coöperation than "How is Jesse's toothache today?" If the tooth still aches and the probation officer can say, "I came to ask whether Jesse would not like to go to a dental clinic so this pain may be stopped," he has proven his interest in the child and his ability to get results. Even when other forms of treatment are much more urgent, probation officers often spend the greater part of the first visit discussing the health of the child and what can be done to improve it. In order to attain their ends, they sometimes improperly utilize health treatment as a bribe to win compliance with other demands.

If the advantages of medical treatment are not appreciated or if children and parents will not coöperate because of laziness, unconcern, or unwillingness to spend money, the Court sometimes uses threats or force. In some cases where the child was apparently behaving in a commendable manner, a tonsillectomy or the filling of teeth was made prerequisite for the termination of probation. Sometimes the probation officer threatened to report parents to the judge, to fine them, or to "send the child away" if the treatment recommended was not permitted. A more successful method was to require that all physical recommendations be fulfilled before sending the child to camp, to the beach, or on a vacation in the country. This method worked especially well if an application blank were given to the parents to sign and the physical requirements plainly stated. In some instances probation officers shamed the parents into permitting or requiring treatment. Another method less frequently used was to interest parents in their children's health by inviting them to see gymnasium demonstrations where awards were given for perfect health, and to see health poster exhibits.

A corollary of health work proved to be emphasis on personal appearance as affected by cleanliness and care of clothes. Pride in white teeth, well cared for hair and finger-nails, and neatness of clothing, resulted from contacts with probation officers. Miss B. says she considers it her duty to be dressed in attractive and becoming clothes. Her girls often say: "Miss B., you always look so pretty," whereupon Miss B. explains the reason. She attributes her success in many cases to conversations on washable gloves, planning outfits "that match," giving suggestions on arrangement of hair and the cleaning of suede shoes and answering satisfactorily other questions so perplexing to the under-privileged girl.

Reasons Recommendations were not Fulfilled. The reasons for failure to carry out the health recommendations seemed to be lack of coöperation on the part of the parent, lack of effort on the part of the probation officer, lack of facilities, and unwillingness of the child to coöperate. The non-coöperative parents include those who resent the interference of the Court because they "do not need anyone to tell them how to raise their children"; ignorant parents, who do not realize the dangers in incipient diseases, or who have superstitious fears of hospitals and of doctors; easy-going parents who are willing that the recommendations be carried out but who lack the intelligence or perseverance to make appointments and to see that their children keep them; parents who are unwilling to spend money on doctors' bills but who give other excuses for their actions. Children who refuse to see doctors, to have operations, or to take medicine usually are prompted by fear, either of the pain or unpleasantness involved, or of unknown terrors, relics of their early training when doctors were placed in the same category as the "bogeyman."

In cases where the probation officer did not urge treatment, the following conditions were found to exist: the case was filed; the court accepted the diagnosis of a family physician who said that the Clinic's recommendations were not imperative; an appointment was made but was not followed up; responsibility for the child's health was left to the parents.

In most cases "lack of facilities" is synonymous with "lack of funds," especially where contact with free clinics was not made. In a few cases the maladies were considered outside the range of present medical science, as for example, some cases of glandular disturbance.

Outcome in Relation to Physical Health. Although the percentage of success on probation is higher for both boys and girls among the persons whose physical recommendations were fulfilled, there is little evidence of a direct relationship between conduct and health. The indication is rather that persons who coöperated with the probation officer in matters of discipline and in carrying out other instructions also coöperated in matters of health.

It is possible to trace a relationship between physical defect and disease and poor strength, lack of ambition, nervousness, and irritability. These in turn may be contributing factors to delinquency since they bring about defensive and compensatory types of behavior. However, the correction of the ailment does not automatically solve the problem since it does not restore to a normal state the mental and social attitudes of the individual. Hence the all-important problem is the prevention of physical inadequacy. This involves a larger public health program putting into operation the principles of public and personal health already established and utilizing the facilities at hand.

It should not be necessary for the probation officer to spend his time taking children to and from hospitals to have their tonsils extracted, and in arguing with parents over the advisability of allowing special treatment for tubercular children. If the time expended by the probation officers on health problems could have been spent on other types of treatment, there would perhaps have been a higher percentage of success among the 500 children.

THE MENTAL AND EMOTIONAL LIFE OF 500 JUVENILE DELINQUENTS

By the arbitrary limitations set in the selection of case material, the 500 children studied were all sane. That is, the investigator excluded persons definitely known to be suffering from a mental disease—those described legally as "insane" and medically as "psychotic." But just as it is sometimes difficult to distinguish between physical health and physical illness, so it is likewise difficult to distinguish between mental health and mental illness. One individual suffering from a broken arm may be incapacitated while another with the same kind of injury may proceed about his business apparently without heeding his affliction. In the same way a slight mental aberration may disrupt the entire social organization of one individual and make him incompetent to maintain himself in society, while for another individual the same type of aberration would not interfere with the daily routine. Since no clear line of demarcation exists between the mentally sound and the mentally unsound, any sample of the population will contain some persons falling in the border zone. Both degree of abnormality and the effect of the particular defect or "quirk" in one's activities must be considered in making a diagnosis.

A considerable number of the children studied show symptoms of mental disorder or of emotional disturbance so pronounced as to lead to abnormal behavior. Only ten children (six boys and four girls) were during their probation period diagnosed as "abnormal"; [2] and thirty others (twenty-eight boys and two girls) revealed abnormal tendencies.[3] In addition to these forty persons, 167 others (127 boys and 40 girls) normal in personality seemed to have unwholesome inner mental life.

As behavior is considered only a symptom of an internal state, it is essential to discover what lies behind it. By eliciting from the child his "own story" the psychiatrist finds out the forces motivating behavior. In discussing the values of this technique, Dr. Healy says:

"In our best studies of delinquents we venture to commend what we call 'Own Story,' and we especially value the psychologist or psychiatrist skilled in getting this. Of course, the delinquent is not always readily articulate, sometimes the study of the inner mental life is obtained with great difficulty, occasionally not at all. But upon the obtaining of it sometimes has certainly depended success or failure of outcome.

"One of the chief regrets of my earlier work in Chicago is that

[2] This group includes those diagnosed by the Clinic according to recent classification as "constitutionally inferior personality," "peculiar or idiosyncratic personality," and "unstable-egocentric personality." Healy, William; Clark, Éric K.; and Kasanin, Jacob, "A Study of Abnormal Personalities." (A paper presented at the International Mental Hygiene Conference, Washington, 1930.)

[3] No attempt is made here to interpret delinquency in psychoanalytic terms. The expressions used aim only at a description of the personality characteristics and emotional reactions of these delinquents.

I never gave time enough or was not skillful enough to get at the inner mental life of a capable boy who appeared over and over in the juvenile court, tight-lipped, always reticent to an extreme, and even in his physiognomy giving evidence of repressing something; a boy who was given most unusual chances in friendship and employment, but whose "Own Story" was never obtained by any of us; a boy who steadily set his path in anti-social ways, despite suffering and punishment, until he became a typical professional criminal —now for years in and out of adult correctional institutions with, undoubtedly, the old sore spot still unexplored, covered up, but remaining the original agent in his career. One thinks of him in contrast to others, where the direct approach to mental life definitely unearthed some similarly potent feature of experience and reaction, and this gave rationally and at once a check to delinquency." [4]

Centuries before the origin of child guidance clinics and long before child psychology became a popular discipline, parents and educators were concerned with the thoughts and ideals of children. Children were urged to read stories of heroism, to see plays picturing ideal characters, and to hear the praises of virtues in order that their thoughts might be noble, lofty, and pure. On the other hand, children were protected from things that are low, obscene, sinful, debasing, and hideous in order that their minds might not be contaminated. Purity of thought has always been believed to lead to good conduct.

This study bears witness to the truth of this conception. Almost one-fifth of all the children (sixty-eight boys and twenty-eight girls) reveal through their "own story" sex ideation or criminal ideation as a "causative factor" in delinquency. The origin of this ideation can be traced back to environmental situations: poor neighborhoods, where vice and crime are omnipresent; poor home conditions and standards, overcrowding, and inadequate sleeping arrangements; drunkenness and poverty; movies portraying criminals as heroes; and tabloid newspapers featuring sensational articles on sex affairs, "love nests," graft and gangster life; unfortunate ex-

[4] Healy, William, "The Psychology of the Situation," *The Child, The Clinic and the Court*, p. 45.

periences of the child resulting from his association with bad companions or from his being prey to unscrupulous men and women. The importance of knowing both the external situations and also the individual's reactions to them is constantly made apparent; for it is only by analyzing the total situation that the causes of misbehavior can be understood and the adjustment of the individual attained.

A somewhat smaller group (fifty-nine boys and twelve girls) showed evidences of "conflict" or of "complexes" that had resulted in conduct disorders. Conflict arising within family relationships appear most frequently. "Inferiority complexes" rank next in order. The remainder of the children showed emotional disturbance due to a deep sense of guilt over various matters. The following list gives the number of boys and girls presenting each type of mental or emotional problem:

Factors of Mental Life	Boys	Girls	Total
Abnormal personalities.............	6	4	10
Abnormal reactions..................	28	2	30
Criminal ideation....................	32	12	44
Disturbing sex ideation.............	36	16	52
Conflict over family situation..........	26	7	33
Inferiority feelings	23	1	24
Guilt feelings.......................	10	4	14
Total	161	46	207

All of these children appear in the lists of persons whose delinquency was attributed to "subjective causations." In them are discovered inner problems, response to situations that have prevented normal emotional development; mental conflict and emotional disturbances due to shocks, injustices, or cruelty. They present a striking contrast to an almost equal number of delinquents whose misconduct is due to unrestrained impulses and the uninhibited expression of desires—children whose inadequate training has not compelled them to develop self-control or whose inferior mental ability renders them unable to anticipate the results of their behavior.

THE TREATMENT OF UNDESIRABLE ATTITUDES AND EMOTIONAL STATES

Problems originating in attitudes and emotions are infinitely more complicated for the probation officer to deal with than problems arising directly from environmental conditions. When a child's delinquency is said to result from lack of constructive recreational interests, clubs, games, and books may be supplied. At least there is something tangible to attempt. The community offers numerous resources for attaining this end. But when the child's problems are attributed to an "inferiority complex" or to "sex ideation as a result of unfortunate experiences" there is no stereotyped solution. The facilities for treatment are necessarily limited because few people understand the significance of satisfactory mental and emotional life. Parents and even educators are not aware of the devastating effects on the child of fear, of a sense of failure, of shame, and of a recognition of inadequacy. Nor do they sufficiently appreciate the necessity for achievement, affectional response, and a feeling of security. A probation officer can indicate to a mother the harm resulting from companionship with a bad boy or girl in the neighborhood; but he finds it difficult to persuade her that her own scoldings and harshness or her overindulgence is the cause of the child's abnormal reactions to his life situation.

Unfortunately the records of the probation officer contain very little statement of aim, process, or result of their more confidential contacts with the child. Whereas the Clinic records give in many cases verbatim accounts of the conversation, the Court records give only brief mention that a conversation took place. For example:

"Tried to show girl the unreasonableness of her present attitude toward her stepfather."

"Boy seems to be developing some self-respect. His attitude has been different ever since the probation officer persuaded him to break away from the C. Street gang."

The increasing tendency of both Court and Clinic to emphasize the subjective factors in delinquency is apparent. Yet in a large part of all the records attention is directed entirely to objective factors.

The Clinic proves to be practically the only agency of psychiatric treatment. Its work begins with the very first contact. As the psychologist and psychiatrist interview the children and their parents, they interpret these individuals to themselves. By encouraging children and parents to express their grievances, their fears, their hatreds, and ambitions, the psychiatrist helps them to an understanding of their own behavior and of the behavior of others.

But in addition to the incidental mental therapy given to all clients, it was possible to return one-fifth of all the boys and girls to the Clinic for special treatment. Ten boys and two girls were given intensive psychiatric treatment by the Clinic's psychiatrists and two boys were treated by private psychiatrists. Thirty-seven boys and nine girls returned for sex instruction and for help in the development of rational attitudes toward sex in order to correct or to counteract their distorted ideas. The psychiatrists had additional conferences with twenty-one boys and six girls regarding their reactions to parents and to other members of the family. The remaining thirteen boys and eight girls were advised regarding their work, school, recreation, or health. In twenty other cases parents came back to the Clinic voluntarily to request advice in dealing with other children.

Most of the cases of sex ideation, and conflict and inferiority feeling resulting from sex experiences received treatment. These troubles arise partly from fear of injurious physical and mental effects and partly from "uneasiness" and consciousness of being "different" due to violation of the mores. Usually one or two contacts with the psychiatrist are sufficient to convince a child that his sex practices can be and should be corrected. But often persistent effort is necessary to modify deleterious habits. Supplying substitutive interests proved a solution for many of these young people and for those described as having "delinquent ideation." In some cases removal from the home was necessary because parents were unable or unwilling to provide suitable surroundings and to give proper supervision and "moral support." The average probation term for the 207 children with delinquent ideation or emotional disturbances was more than twice that of the children whose problems were more overt. This fact alone indicates that these problems are more difficult to cope with or that the probation officer is less skilled in their treatment. Analysis of the records indicates that both conditions play a part.

Of the ten persons diagnosed as "abnormal personalities," six were permanent successes and only two, failures. The favorable outcome of these cases, however, was possible only because in addition to the supervision of the probation officer each child was given long and intensive treatment by the Clinic or other social agencies. The outcome of the other thirty children with "abnormal reactions," whose defects were not so pronounced as in the above group and who did not receive special treatment, is quite different. One-half of these children were surrendered to the Court as failures, the probation officer admitting his inability to deal with them. Of the remainder, one-half repeated their delinquency within a few months after probation ended, and at present only three children, or about one-tenth of the persons with personality difficulties, are making a satisfactory adjustment to their home and neighborhood groups.

While the number is not large, it indicates rather clearly that probation officers cannot be expected to give a sufficient amount of psychotherapeutic treatment for persons exhibiting abnormal personality traits. For these cases the intensive treatment of a psychiatrist or of a psychiatric case worker seems necessary.

Table IX shows the relative amount of success for each group. The boys and girls with abnormal grudges, fears, obsessions, and inferiority feelings seem to be less hopeful than those whose criminal ideation or disturbing sex ideation led them into delinquency.

TABLE IX

Outcome in relation to mental and personality factors

	Success	Tempo-rary Success	Failure	Unknown	Total
Abnormal personality....	6	2	2		10
Abnormal reactions......	3	12	14	1	30
Disturbing ideation......	63	24	20	3	110
Family conflict..........	11	7	14	1	33
Inferiority feelings......	9	6	8	1	24
Total	92	51	58	6	207

Of the entire 207 children whose mental content or emotional reactions deviated from the normal, the percentage of failure (28 per cent) was more than double the percentage of failure (13 per cent) for the remaining 293 children. Likewise the proportion of temporary success was greater for the former, and the interval between offenses shorter.

SUMMARY AND CONCLUSIONS

Clinic examination of 500 children shows many defects needing attention. For one out of every ten children a physical recommendation was important. On the other hand, few persons were in perfect physical condition; more than three-fourths of all the children had carious teeth, diseased or enlarged tonsils, poor posture, or other minor defects. According to numerous studies the physical condition of these children is similar to that of other children from the same homes and neighborhoods.

The Clinic's interpretation of physical status and its significance is an important part of treatment. The probation officer also spends much time in trying to give parents and children an appreciation of the importance of good health. In dealing with health problems, the probation officer cannot himself give treatment. In securing medical attention, he relies to a great extent upon the coöperation of school nurses, social service departments of hospitals, and upon free clinics.

Although only one-half the total number of recommendations were carried out, more than one-half of all children received medical attention through the efforts of the probation officers. The chief reasons for failure to fulfill recommendations are: (1) the parents resented court interference in matters of health; and (2) facilities for free treatment were lacking.

Physical defects may indirectly cause delinquency, but their correction does not automatically eliminate the delinquency.

Almost two-fifths of all children exhibited personality or emotional reactions sufficiently "abnormal" to indicate a need for mental hygiene. No child definitely psychotic ("insane") was placed on probation, but a few children during the course of the probation terms were diagnosed as having psychotic tendencies. The "own story" proved to be a valuable technique for discovering abnormal tendencies.

Facilities for mental hygiene are extremely limited, the Judge Baker Foundation being the main agency in Boston consistently used by the probation officers in the treatment of delinquent children. In some cases only one or two interviews were needed to bring about a change of reaction or attitude; in other cases prolonged treatment was necessary. The adjustment of personality problems is especially difficult because parents very often do not understand their origin and significance and therefore are not willing to coöperate in the proper treatment of them. This is particularly true of problems arising from unhappy home situations.

The average probation term of children with delinquent ideation and emotional disturbances was twice that of children with normal reactions. In spite of the longer term the percentage of failure in the former group was double that of the latter. It seems apparent, therefore, that probation officers not trained in psychiatric case work are unable to solve personality problems. A closer coördination of the work of the clinic and the court seems advisable.

CHAPTER V

PROBATION AND COMPANIONSHIP

"Juvenile delinquency" usually connotes group activity and not lone individuals secretly (or even openly) engaging in anti-social behavior. When a rock crashes through a window, the owner of the building starts in pursuit of "some little devils." When a fruit vender finds his wagon overturned, he says, "I'll get the rascals." In general, certainly, this is true. Because of the tendency for evil doers to work in pairs or groups it is extremely important to analyze, first, the part companions play in the motivation or expression of behavior; second, the work of the probation officer in handling companionship problems; and third, the relative efficacy of various methods of treatment.

EXTENT OF DELINQUENT COMPANIONSHIP

Fortunately the number of sources through which both subjective and objective data regarding companionship could be gathered was very great; and each provided unusual opportunity to secure abundant material. Chief among the sources of information are the child's own accounts of his companions: first, as given at the time of his arrest to the police officer, the judge, the probation officer, the complainant, and his parents; later, as told during his examination and treatment at the Clinic to psychologist, psychiatrist, and social worker; and finally, the child's evaluations of his past experiences as confided in retrospect to the probation officer, the Judge Baker Foundation follow-up visitor, and the psychiatrists or headmasters at state training schools.

The opinions of parents and other members of the family

on the matter of the child's companions and their influence were elicited by the same agencies as listed above, but do not necessarily correspond to the data given by the children.

Other sources of information within the community are: police officers on the beat; probation and parole officers of the companions; club leaders; schoolteachers and principals; priests and ministers; complainants; employers; neighbors, including the parents of companions; and social workers.

Detailed sociological analyses were made of several representative groups. The writer's study of the gang called "Cantons" involved conferences with forty-six persons. The study of the "Tilestons" gang, who were all Italians, was made by a case worker of that nationality, well known and much loved in that district.[1]

Only 19 per cent of the boys and 13 per cent of the girls acknowledged associating with bad companions or being influenced in their misbehavior by bad companions. The boys especially tended to assume responsibility for their actions. When asked, "Who suggested that you take that automobile?" or "Whose idea was it that you break open the cash drawer?" a majority of the boys would reply, "We all thought of it" or "We just did it—we didn't plan to," thus refraining from placing the blame on any one person. They often reply in this manner because of a code of honor that prevents "squealing." Many children when telling their stories, contend that their playmates are "good" boys and girls, but their evaluations are based upon very low standards. Only nine boys and seven girls expressed any bitterness toward companions who had used them as tools or who had drawn them into wrong doing without warning them of the dangers. However, almost all of the children (87 per cent of the boys and 75 per cent of the girls) stated that they knew boys and girls who were bad, though they would not admit to close association with them.

It is perhaps noteworthy that the parents knew very little

[1] Miss Elizabeth Balch financed the project and secured the services of this excellent investigator, thus insuring a type of coöperation from parents, the children themselves, and other social workers that could scarcely have been secured by an American social worker.

about the companions of their children. The mothers who worked away from home knew no less than those who did not. If boys and girls had been giving trouble by staying out late at night, by "bunking" away from home, or by truanting (to the extent that school authorities visited the home), parents assumed that this waywardness must be caused by bad companions; but even then less than one-half of them could give the name of any specific person who was to blame. In forty-seven instances, however, they pointed definitely to the bad influence of individuals. Of these, forty-one had known for as long as two months that their children had undesirable associates and had been trying to break up the companionships.

The record of the Court offers objective evidence of bad companionship. The Court asks the question: "With whom was the child when he committed the offense for which he is in court?" The answer is:

> One hundred and four boys and thirty-four girls were alone and apparently acting upon their own initiative.
>
> Twenty boys and twenty girls were alone when they committed the offense but they acted at the instigation of another person.
>
> Forty-three boys and sixteen girls were with one companion.
>
> Two hundred and thirty-three boys and thirty girls were with two or more companions.

Thus it is apparent that three-fourths of the group had associates in their misbehavior.

The Clinic as well as the Court records the names of companions. By listing all the persons whose names were found in either place, and clearing them through the Massachusetts Probation Commission, the investigator learned how many were caught delinquent. Their court numbers were then recorded on the schedules of the children studied. These cross references show clearly the tendency of "birds of a feather" to "flock together." All except 8 per cent of the boys and 10 per cent of the girls had cross references indicating "bad companions." These associates may be designated "bad" only in the legal sense, the term meaning that they have been arraigned in court and given a verdict of "delinquent" by the judge. A cross reference does not necessarily mean that the bad companion referred to has exerted harmful influence on the child studied. On the other hand, this list certainly does not contain the names of all persons who have contributed to the child's delinquency. Perhaps the most dangerous persons through cleverness or the subtlety of their influence have escaped scrutiny.

When all the foregoing reports have been summarized, only twenty-four boys and nine girls had no records of bad companionship. In all these cases their parents reported "good" companions. Nine boys and six girls had no companions of their own age. All others except these forty-eight had been associating to more or less degree with delinquents.

COMPANIONS AS INSTIGATORS OF DELINQUENCY

Having discovered that the delinquent child has in most cases companions who are also delinquent, the probation officer next asks, "To what extent were the companions responsible for the misbehavior of the child?" An answer demands thorough consideration of the entire physical, mental, and emotional make-up of all the children concerned. It involves a careful weighing and balancing one against another of intricate and sometimes almost intangible factors. The types of companionship association may be classified roughly under three headings:

1. "Bad companion causative" is the term used when there is evidence that the child's misbehavior is due to the example, suggestions, or demand of a specific person or persons, of or near his own age.
2. "Companionship affair" is an expression implying acts committed with others that would not be committed alone. This category includes many mischievous affairs such as ringing alarms, setting fires, breaking windows, tripping passersby, and more serious offenses such as entering buildings, pilfering and robbery. It means that the behavior is engaged in by all the group and that all are more or less at fault. Such escapades

are generally not planned, but are guided by the inspiration of the moment.

3. "Instigation of older person" describes the causal relationship in the cases of the children who are initiated into sex affairs by sex perverts, and the children who steal articles at the request of "fences" who pay them a minimum sum for their trouble.

The extent to which each of these kinds of association operated is shown by the following summary:

JUDGE BAKER FOUNDATION STATEMENT OF CAUSATION

	BOYS	GIRLS	TOTAL
1. Bad companion...................	167	31	198
2. Companionship affair............	111	13	124
3. Instigation of older person........	34	20	54
	312	64	376
Companions not causative........	88	36	124
Total	400	100	500

The following illustrations of the first type are actual samples of cases dealt with by the probation officer. The story of Gilly, for example, shows the far reaching but not fully recognized influence of one bad boy.

Gilly was first known to the court when he was seven and a half years old. He was arrested with two older boys for "breaking and entering, and larceny." He was told by his companions to break a window in an antique shop on Charles Street in order that his companions might get an old sword on display. Being in fear of them, Gilly complied, and all were arrested. Gilly was sent to the Judge Baker Foundation for study. Many important facts were brought to light. Gilly was large for his age, excellently developed, and full of energy and fun. His general intelligence as shown by a battery of tests was considerably above normal. The history of his early childhood was normal in every way. His mother states that he was a happy, sweet, obedient child, until he went to school and was teased because of his "cross-eyes." Several times he had cried bitterly when he came running home from school to evade his schoolmates. Gilly discovered that older boys were less cruel; and sought their company, doing all kinds of errands for them to ingratiate himself with them. Being allowed to associate with the "big fellers" gave him prestige (at least in his own eyes), and he began to assume a lordly attitude toward his own classmates, occasionally condescending to tell them what the big boys did and talked about, gradually becoming more and more elaborate and imaginative in his narratives. The smaller boys were especially impressed with Gilly's stories of crooking. His dramatic ability enabled him to convert his court experience into a heroic episode and to describe the thrills of being an "outlaw" in so fascinating a manner that all of his listeners became consumed with the desire to become heroic crooks. Gilly promised to teach them, and for four years was the instigator or at least the inspiration of numberless breaks, petty thievings, and other crimes. Although there is no evidence that Gilly had ever engaged in sex affairs since he was five years old (when he was taught mutual practices by a boarder), he told his companions many stories of his fabricated experience and seemed to get a great deal of pleasure from inducing other boys to experiment.

In the meantime, Gilly's case was filed in court, as he had complied with all the demands made by the probation officer: he had ceased to associate with the older boys with whom he was arrested; his school grades were satisfactory; he joined a club at a settlement; he did not play on the street after eight o'clock at night; he reported to the probation officer regularly and promptly. He appeared a normal, happy boy.

The following extracts from Judge Baker Foundation records indicate his subtle influence for bad:

Own story of Abraham K.:

"Sure, I know Gilly. He's a regular guy. He has done more robbing than any one in West End. He knows how to rob under your nose and not get caught. He told us how to get the peaches, only John made a noise and we got caught."

Psychiatrist's interview with Joseph M.:

"When asked about Gilly B., the boy's face lighted up. Seems to be somewhat in awe of him. Speaks in a rather reverential tone, giving us the idea he looks upon Gilly as a hero. Tells with pride of many of Gilly's exploits."

Own story of Charles S.:

"I just bunked once, but Gilly says you ain't a man until you have bunked ten times. He has already bunked a hundred times. He bunks with girls, too."

Judge Baker Foundation Summary—Erino P.:

"This little fellow's stealing seems to be due entirely to the influence of a boy whom he calls 'Gilly.' This matter should be investigated."

Mother of Max F. at Judge Baker Foundation:

"I can't do nothing with Max since he has been hanging around with that cross-eyed boy on B. Street. He'll go without his lunch to run out when that fellow whistles. I yell at him but he don't pay me no mind at all."

Own story of Max:

"Oh, Gilly, yes, he is a good guy. He's got brains. He don't get you in trouble the way them C. Street guys do. He knows all the cops. He shook hands with one. I saw him. He tells us how to crook 'tonic' and papers and money from slot machines and how to 'fish' drunks. I'm his pal so he lets me keep half the money when he shows me a drunk to 'fish.' "

Judge Baker Foundation Conference Summary of Stanley K.:

"It seems from this boy's story that Gilly B. is at the root of all the recent breaks in the West End. We long ago recommended that this clever mischief-maker should have some deterrent treatment. Officer claims there is no evidence upon which to arrest him. He never takes any part in any of the breaks and, so far as he can tell, never receives any of the booty."

"Companionship affairs" fall into two classes; those in which the delinquency is more or less spontaneous when it is incited by a peculiarly tempting situation and not directly attributable to any one participant. The case of Mary G. illustrates this type:

"Our mothers sent us to town with ten cents each. We decided that we would buy things instead of going to movies. Since we couldn't buy all the things we wanted, we decided to go to the five-

and-ten and see how much we could get without spending any money. It was great sport for we all thought it was fun and tried to see who could get the most things."

The second type of companionship affair can be traced to neighborhood standards and the mores of the particular group in which the child is reared.

Children of parents transplanted from rural Europe to a congested district where 87,000 persons are encompassed within one square mile, are naturally confused. In order to break down the isolation that threatens to swamp them, they imitate the behavior of the people around them. Unfortunately some of these patterns derive from delinquent companions. What is sometimes referred to as their "contamination" is, sociologically speaking, perhaps only "acclimation." A further amount of the "delinquency" of immigrant youth is not intentional violation of the law, but is due to a misconception of the limits of individual freedom in America.

Benino Agato was reported by his parents to have been "a perfect child" when they lived in the country near Rome. They left their relatives and friends in Italy and came to America chiefly because they wanted Benino to have a chance in this 'Land of Opportunity.' For a while after they moved to the North End he behaved all right, he stayed in the house and read or played with his little sister. After he began to sell papers, he spent less and less time at home, preferring to stay out with other boys who sold papers. One day he noticed that Mike, who always had lots of money, did not get any papers in his own name, but waited until the delivery truck dumped the papers at the central stand and then swiped a few from other bundles when their owners were not looking. Benino tried this and was successful. He found this an easy way to make some extra money, as he was forced by his parents to turn in to them all he earned on the papers he ordered. One night he was invited by some newsies to go riding. For many nights thereafter he went with these boys who "borrowed" automobiles and took rides, sometimes returning them and sometimes leaving them on nearby streets. He refused to tell his parents where or how he spent his evenings, because he feared they would curtail his newfound freedom. He was encouraged at school to choose his own vocation and not to feel that he must follow his father's trade. But unfortunately he interpreted the freedom offered by America to mean license to do as he pleased in all matters.

It is equally difficult for the child who has been born and reared in a district where there is much disregard for law to develop into a law-abiding citizen. The practice of his companions and not the legal code is his standard.

Gaetana says, "I don't see why I can't sell lemons when everybody else does. Carlo ain't got no license either—nor Joe, nor Tony. Why do you pick on me?"

Peter's lips curled when told that it was "not right" to keep change which purchasers would be induced to forget. He said, "H'm! You'd make a h—— of a lot selling papers if you gave everyone back the right change! Do you know anyone who don't keep the change if he can get by with it? I ask you, do you?"

Among the 500 children, there were fifty-four of the third type whose delinquency was due to unscrupulous people to whom they had fallen prey. Included in this group are:

Mary P., who was sold by her mother to a "cadet" for the sum of $100, was brought from Canada to the United States and forced into white slavery.

Simon L. was forced by his mother to sell lemons to get money to buy his own clothes, yet she refused to allow him to apply for a peddling license.

Ruby G. was taught shoplifting by an older companion who promised to teach her to run an embroidery machine if she would get her ten pairs of stockings from Filene's. Ruby had almost earned her tuition when she was arrested.

Richard S. worked on a milk wagon and gave his pay envelope to the neighbors with whom his parents left him when they moved to California. Not satisfied with his small pay, the foster mother suggested to Richard that he should bring home a quart of milk each day, using the argument, "Why work for a dairy if you aren't going to have milk to drink yourself?"

Mary K. was told by a neighbor, Mrs. R., that her sister was going to be married and she would invite Mary to the wedding if she would help her get her trousseau. Mary agreed and went with

Mrs. R. on numerous expeditions to town to get négligée, shoes, scarves and accessories. One day when the trousseau was almost complete, Mrs. R. sent Mary alone to get a pair of white gloves for the bride; but Mary fumbled and was taken to court.

John E. was tempted by the kindly treatment, generous commissions, and exciting life offered by a blind man to leave his home to become his "aide." In the morning John dressed his boss as a beggar, took him to a good, busy corner and spent the day rattling a rusty tin can, and telling pitiful stories of the blind man's poverty. At night he took him home, banked his "beggings" and dressed the boss in full dress preparatory to dining out or going to the theatre. John loved the excitement of a double life, but he also seemed to be genuinely fond of the old man.

From the point of view of breakdown of morale, there is no type of misconduct so dangerous as engaging in sex perversions.

David F. was a lively, imaginative, well developed boy of fifteen. Since he was especially "hard on his clothes," an arrangement was made with a tailor that David should work for him after school to earn a new "Sunday suit." The tailor, Mr. Z., proved to be an unprincipled man who entertained David by showing him obscene pictures and telling lewd stories. Later he taught him perversions, keeping David at the shop after the others had gone. David became so involved that he thought of little else. David told Mr. Z. that his mother objected to his staying at the shop late at night. Mr. Z. gave him some powders to put in her coffee at night so she would get sleepy and go to bed and not know when he came in. Mrs. F. became very ill and David, overcome with remorse and shame, ran away from home.

PROBATION TREATMENT

The probation officer had for a guide in treating each of these problems the Clinic's advice. The recommendations in regard to companions may be classified as prohibitive and constructive. The Clinic prescribed the former for 145 boys and 21 girls, and the latter for 62 boys and 10 girls. The term prohibitive is used to designate those stated in terms of undesirable relationships to be discontinued, as for example:

"Companionship with Hank L. should be broken up immediately. If the bad companion is not sent to Lyman, the family should move from the neighborhood, as the boy himself admits there is no possibility of his going straight as long as he is near Hank."

"This gang which has been involved in so much mischief and now is getting into very bad practices must be broken up. The whole neighborhood situation should be investigated not only for the sake of these boys but for others who are in danger of being drawn in."

"She must not be allowed to associate with the Hyman girl, who has been exerting such a bad influence over her."

The recommendations are termed constructive that are stated in terms of the condition to be achieved, as for example:

"The probation officer should help connect Ralph with better companions. This boy has good abilities and ambitions, and it is a pity for him to waste his time with the fellows on his street. Perhaps Mr. M. at the Y might be persuaded to take an interest in Ralph and introduce him to some decent young men."

"Helen states that she has never had a chum—that she used to pray every night for God to send her a girl friend, who would 'cry when she cried and laugh when she laughed.' Helen's family relationships should be investigated further, but certainly a fundamental need is that of companionship of her own age. It seems that the mother has discouraged Helen's making friends—has never allowed her to bring children to her home, has always taken Helen to school and gone after her, because she has to cross the tracks, and has never allowed her to play on the street. The probation officer should make the mother see the unwisdom of such a policy and enlist her coöperation in establishing normal friendships. If there are no desirable girls in the immediate neighborhood, perhaps Mrs. C. at Little House, or Helen's teacher, who professes an interest in the child, could help."

The difference between the two types is not one of ultimate aim, but of procedure. "Constructive" recommendations constitute long-time plans; "prohibitive" recommendations, immediate action. The former may be compared to the process of growing an oak tree, the latter to chopping it down. After bad companions are eliminated, the probation officer should attempt to supply good ones; this goal is implied in all treatment, though the immediate step to be stressed is only the getting rid of the bad influence. Two factors have to be considered in dealing with companions; namely, parental control and the harmful effects of the companionship. Where parents give normal supervision and have the respect of their children, they may be expected to coöperate in helping the child to meet and cultivate a higher type of friend; but where parents have not had enough interest or intelligence to give their children normal protection and guidance, the probation officer seldom depends upon them to assist in carrying out "constructive" recommendations. Even though they do not appreciate the advantages of superior contacts, they must be impressed with the dangers of bad associations and must be required to protect their children from vicious influences.

Likewise "constructive" plans are proposed where the gang is engaged in mischief affairs and in misdemeanors of a mild sort; but when a child's companion demands that he appropriate automobiles, or induces him into sex perversions, or arouses in him antagonism against his parents or against organized society, it becomes necessary that the association be cut short.

The child's preliminary contacts with the Court and with the Clinic help to pave the way for the choice of new associates and the discarding of old ones. The experience of being interrogated leads the child to examine his friends critically, and to evaluate them in the light of community standards. He sees their crimes exposed and learns why certain of their acts are not legally or socially acceptable. He may feel isolated because of the disapproval expressed by his family and may be willing to relinquish all external contacts in order to be reinstated at home. But often in spite of insight, drastic measures alone succeed in accomplishing anything.

The probation officers attempted to fulfill more than three-fourths of the 238 companionship recommendations (163 for boys, and 25 for girls), and to break up the bad associations of nine other boys, whose friendships developed after the Judge Baker Foundation examination. If these nine are added, the total becomes 247 persons needing this treatment. In 101 instances among the boys and in twelve instances among the girls, a very drastic demand was made, namely, that the child's relations with specified individuals be terminated. This plan is called drastic because in many cases the companionship was of long duration and the children lived in close proximity. Friends are somewhat like habits, they cannot be discarded by a gesture or merely by expressing a desire to be rid of them. Prohibitions and threats had usually already been tried by parents; prohibitions and threats of probation officers were consequently of little avail. No probation officer can be constantly with his probationers to keep them away from their undesirable playmates; hence other motives or methods must be employed.

The methods used to effect a break of the gang were: "removal" of the bad companion, especially if he were the leader (usually by commitment to a training school or by foster home placement); the removal of the child from his home (either by foster home placement or by sending him on a vacation to a camp or to relatives or friends); or by the removal of the child's family from the neighborhood to a more desirable location. In other words, the most effective method of achieving social separation of children is by the expedient of geographic separation.

Where bad companionship is not an emergency problem, two other methods were successfully used. The first may be called "substitutive activities," which include keeping the child away from his old associates by occupying his time with pleasures in which they cannot be included and redirecting the entire group so that they engage in constructive pastimes. The chapters dealing with recreation, school, and work suggest instances where this type of treatment was employed. The second type of treatment is referred to as "moral suasion." It includes threats, scoldings, pleadings, and admonitions and also encouragement and advice. The threats and scoldings brought temporary results by instilling fear or guilt feelings into the child. The inspiration and encouragement, though not frequent or conspicuous, showed more lasting results. The methods used in breaking up undesirable friendships are listed below:

Methods Used	Boys	Girls	Total
Send companion away	35	0	35
Send child away	47	8	55
Move to a new neighborhood	19	4	23
Substitutive activities	36	3	39
Moral suasion	26	10	36
Total	163	25	188

OUTCOME IN RELATION TO COMPANIONSHIP

There is least hope for success with boys and girls who, though knowing bad companions, are "lone hands" in their delinquencies. Only 42 per cent of them were successfully handled on probation. The offenders who plan and execute their crimes alone show in almost all cases the development of criminalistic attitudes and habits that are not easily eradicated. The leaders of small groups are slightly more hopeful than persons who do not seek support. The boys who were accompanied by one companion show 65 per cent success as compared with 70 per cent for those involved in "crowd" affairs. All treatment where delinquencies were instigated by others was successful. Of the children who had never had any bad companions, 80 per cent were successes.

The outcome of probation for girls seems to be more definitely dependent upon the two factors that have been mentioned before, namely, parental control and early sex experience. If the girl's companionships were linked up with sex affairs with the opposite sex, probation offered no remedy.

The probation officer is more successful in dealing with the companionship problems of younger than of older children. Table X shows the extent to which the Clinic recommendations were carried out for the different age groups.

Sending the leader (the bad companion) away acts as a deterrent to delinquency in two ways. It is a warning to other children and to parents, and, chiefly, it removes the bad influ-

TABLE X

Age in relation to fulfillment of Judge Baker Foundation
recommendations regarding companionship

Age of Child	Total Number of Recommendations	Percentage of Recommendations		
		Fulfilled	Attempted but not fulfilled	Not attempted
7 yrs. to 10 yrs. 6 mos.	41	83	12	5
10 yrs. 6 mos. to 13 yrs. 6 mos. ...	82	60	16	24
13 yrs. 6 mos. to 17 yrs.	93	56	20	24
Total	216	62	17	21

ence from the associates remaining. In 90 per cent of the cases
the other fellow's punishment acted as a temporary check.
However, 50 per cent of the boys repeated their delinquency
within six months after probation ended, whereas only 24 per
cent of the persons whose misbehavior was corrected by "substitutive activities" were recidivists. In the case of Guano C.,
removal of his companion led to more, not less, crime.

Guano C. and his friend Harry had been in several "breaks"
together. Finally Harry, who was on suspended sentence to Lyman,
was "sent up." Within a week Guano repeated the very same offense
and was also sent to the training school. Later he admitted that they
had made an agreement that if one were caught, the other should
do something to be "sent up." After two years, both boys were
returned to the same neighborhood on parole, and their stealing
episodes were resumed. Both boys are now in the Massachusetts
Reformatory serving five-year sentences.

The chief reason for the probation officer's failure in fifty
cases to attempt to carry out the recommendations of the Judge
Baker Foundation was the uncoöperative attitude of the child.
A fourth of the delinquents refused to report to their probation
officers and evaded the officers' visits. All except one of these
persons were committed to training schools and consequently
are classified as failures. In one-half of the cases, the probation

officer gave his attention entirely to other problems, work, place of living, school, or recreation. The following table makes clear the relation between success and failure and the fulfillment of companionship recommendations:

TABLE XI

*Probation treatment in relation to outcome for boys and girls having companionship recommendations**

	Total Number	Percentage'			
		Success	Tempo-rary Success	Failure	Un-known
Recommendations attempted					
Fulfilled	154	59	35	4	2
Not fulfilled.................	43	11.5	39.5	47	2
Recommendations not attempted	50	32	30	35	2
Total......................	247	45	35	18	2

* This includes also the nine children for whom the probation officer attempted treatment of companionship problems which developed after the clinical examination.

When the probation officer was successful in solving the companionship problems as advised by the Clinic, the percentage of permanent success was 59 as compared with 4 per cent total failure. On the other hand, when the probation officer was not able to separate the child from undesirable associates, the situation was reversed; that is, few were permanent successes (11.5 per cent), while a great many were total failures (47 per cent). When the probation officer did not attempt to change the delinquents' companions, the percentage of success and failure is approximately equal.

This chapter affords abundant evidence of the importance of knowing with whom the delinquent associates and the needs met by this association. This is not surprising when one recalls that a large part of a child's life is normally occupied with his social relationships. The less satisfying the contacts within the family, the more dependent the child becomes upon his playmates, the greater the degree to which his personality is merged in that of the gang, and the more desperate the acts which he commits in order to obtain or retain status in the group.

Bad companions may be sought by a child to satisfy his subconscious desire to punish or to take revenge upon his parents for their oppression (e.g., imposing hard work or long hours, or severe beatings or scoldings); or for their failure to respect the individuality of the child (e.g., by taking his pay envelope); or for their immorality or crime that causes the child to be embarrassed, ashamed, and disgusted. Even a suspicion that his parents are guilty of an offense may cause a child to enter into an orgy of misbehavior.

Joy in the participation of successful adventures is not tempered very noticeably by ideas of moral judgment. The satisfaction derived from devising clever means of entering buildings, the excitement of eluding pursuers, the thrill of carrying off the booty, and finally the pleasure derived from the use of the stolen property—food, clothing, money, weapons, toys, musical instruments, and automobiles—are powerful motives which link together young adventurers and become the ties upon which their friendship is based. The admiration of daring, though unscrupulous, companions leads to much of the reckless delinquency of youth.

When the probation officer came in contact with these children, more than 90 per cent of them had previously been associated with bad companions who, in 75 per cent of the cases, could be considered responsible, directly or indirectly, for their delinquency. This was one of the most important problems with which the probation officer had to deal. Either by separating the child geographically from his bad companions or by providing substitutive satisfying recreations the probation officer was able in 63 per cent of the cases to modify constructively the child's companionship. These results are quite remarkable when one considers that the child's contacts with the probation officer are necessarily limited, whereas his companions are in close and constant proximity. Moreover, it is important to note that where companionship problems were solved, the number of permanently successful cases was fifteen times as great as the failures. Where the treatment of companionship problems was either unsuccessful or not attempted, the successes were only one-half as numerous as the failures.

SUMMARY

Juvenile delinquency is largely a group phenomenon. Nine-tenths of the juvenile delinquents have companions who are also delinquent. Three-fourths of juvenile delinquents commit offenses in the company of others. Parents almost invariably blame the delinquency of their children on bad companions, but show an amazing ignorance regarding the companions of their children.

The remaining one-fourth commit the offenses alone, often at the instigation of an older person. Juvenile delinquents who have no companions and those who commit the offenses alone engage in more serious crimes and are less likely to be successful on probation than those who engage in mischief in gangs.

The Clinic's recommendations with regard to companionship may be classified as "constructive" and "prohibitive." The former demands long-time plans, the latter immediate action, often geographic separation. Constructive treatment can be attempted where there is good parental control and where the child has not been engaging in vicious recreations. Constructive recommendations are fulfilled by substitutive activities and by moving to a better neighborhood. Prohibitive treatment consists largely of threats and the removal of the child from his home.

Younger children are more easily separated from bad companions than older children. For children of all ages action must be immediate. If there is delay, the tie is strengthened.

The percentage of failure was ten times as great among children whose companionship recommendations were not carried out as when they were.

CHAPTER VI

PROBATION AND RECREATION

Students of delinquent children note with great frequency the paucity of their constructive interests and their limited facilities for desirable recreation.[1]

Except for truancy the offenses for which children are referred to court are perpetrated almost entirely during leisure time. This investigation seeks to discover the relationship between delinquency and recreational pursuits and the power of probation to eradicate, decrease, or prevent delinquency by improving the use of leisure time. The investigation resolves itself into four questions: How do delinquent children spend their leisure time? Does leisure spent in poor recreations cause delinquency? What can be done to improve the recreation of children on probation? Does improved recreation improve conduct?

THE RECREATION OF DELINQUENT CHILDREN

The Clinic records contain abundant material concerning the recreational activities of the group. They seem to include, however, only vital interests or conspicuous lack of interests. They do not attempt to give detailed information which might be obtained from a recreation questionnaire.[2] In some cases, several activities were given; in many cases only one or two. The accompanying table shows, in order of frequency, the pastimes reported by 400 boys and 100 girls.

Table XII lists recreations ordinarily considered commend-

[1] Breckinridge, Sophonisba P., *The Delinquent Child and the Home*, pp. 157-158; Burt, Cyril, *The Young Delinquent*, pp. 87-88; Thurston, Henry W., *Delinquency and Spare Time*, pp. 150-152.
[2] Information regarding club membership was verified from the records of the clubs, so this may be considered valid.

TABLE XII

Pastimes of 500 boys and girls

Activities	Boys	Girls	Total
Movies	212	38	250
Reading	187	41	228
Street life	163	22	185
Club membership*	130	28	158
Sports—non-team	119	15	134
Sex play	75	29	104
Sports—organized team	92	0	92
Church	54	12	66
Music	31	15	46
Mechanics	18	0	18
Dancing	7	10	17
Gambling	14	0	14
Drawing and painting	8	6	14
Cards	12	0	12
Pool and billiards	11	0	11
Bunking	11	0	11
Loafing	10	0	10
Beaches	6	4	10
Childish games	4	4	8
Pets	6	0	6
Dramatics	4	2	6
Drinking	5	0	5
Joy riding at night	2	3	5
Total	1181	229	1410

* Twenty-five boys and seven girls are included who were not attending club regularly at the time of their examination, but who had been club members earlier. At first these were recorded separately but since they resembled club members in every respect, they were later classed with them.

able and also those considered pernicious. When the individual's total leisure time activity is analyzed, his recreations may be classified as good, fair, poor, or vicious according to the following criteria:

Good. Recreation to be good must be planned and well supervised and must include some form or forms of leisure time activity recognized as constructive. For example:

Filipo Salvatore is reported as "A lively boy with good recreations and interests. Plays basketball and football. Attends church and Sunday School regularly. He has a library card and enjoys reading good books. Belongs to a club at Elizabeth Peabody House."

Fair. Fair indicates that the child's recreation is partially planned or partially supervised, or that he engages in activities of an innocuous, though not especially constructive type. "Fair" also denotes a balance between desirable and undesirable leisure time activities. No person with any regular pastimes that were definitely vicious would be included.

Nora Frankytes says of her own play life, "Yes, I have a good time. I play on my steps and on my friend's steps. We play dolls, marbles, jacks, and skips and say things to people who pass, and then laugh. Sometimes we play grown-up and walk up and down the block with our heads high. I like to see the lights at night but my papa makes me go to bed at eight o'clock. My friend goes to the movies, but I have not been for over two years. Yes, I love to read funny papers and my friend's book about Alice."

Poor. Time spent in undirected, unsupervised chance activity, such as sitting listening to parents' and neighbors' gossip is classified as poor. A child's recreation is likewise considered poor if he has no time for pleasurable pursuits, or if he spends all his time on the street.

Geoffrey Harris "has no constructive interests. When not in school (and it is difficult to find him there) he plays on the street or in a shack built by him and his companions. They collect junk which they sell for ice cream. A favorite sport is rock throwing.

Geoffrey boasts of many exploits of his gang such as hopping rides, stealing fruit, and teasing a crippled beggar who lives on his street."

Vicious. Activities which are prohibited by law or which border on illegal practices, such as drinking, sex practices, and gambling are classified as vicious.[3]

Julius Freeman "spends his time loafing on the street corners and in the subway station on the Common where he meets men regularly for illegal purposes. He seldom comes home before midnight, going the rounds of several disreputable dance halls every evening. He states that he dislikes reading, but the probation officer reports that Julius always has in his possession magazines of a very low order and several copies of what are known as 'joke books.'"

Age, mental status, physical and social development also help to determine the classifications of the activities described.

No recreation is considered in itself either good or bad, but is rated according to its effect on the child and the community and the extent to which it meets in wholesome fashion his needs and desires. For example, playing the piano is for Maria L. a great joy. She says,

"It is just Heaven to play and practice. I let myself go then; and am happy. The music says things to me and I says things on the piano that I can never say out loud in words."

But to Frances R. the piano is something to be detested, because forced upon her by her mother, who is seeking through her daughter to expand her own ego. In the same way church attendance, reading *Ivanhoe,* and playing football may be desirable amusements under some circumstances and undesirable under others. Differences in sex, racial and cultural differences, and even neighborhood mores helped to determine classification. Several boys rated as having "poor" recreation wandered unchaperoned on the street at night; but as every girl within the study who had habitually "stayed out late" had been immoral, this recreation is considered for the girls "vicious."

[3] Several cases of "excessive movies" are included because in each case movie attendance was made possible by unlawful practices, such as stealing money, truanting, and bunking in movie houses.

When considered in relation to the above classification, only 73 of the 500 delinquents have adequate recreation. For more than five-sixths of the group an improvement of the use of leisure time is needed. If the categories Fair and Poor be combined, 71 per cent of the boys and 63 per cent of the girls lack constructive activities or find their amusement in undesirable ways.

Girls tend to be graded higher in recreation than do boys but sex differences are not significant. Thus, 51 per cent of the girls fall in the categories Good and Fair as compared with 43 per cent of the boys. On the other hand, more girls than boys are included in the Vicious category.

The following list shows the percentage of boys and girls falling in each class:

	PERCENTAGE	
RECREATION GRADE	BOYS	GIRLS
Good	14	16
Fair...........................	28	35
Poor...........................	43	28
Vicious	15	21
Total	100	100

The younger the delinquent the less likely is he to have either very good or very poor recreations. For the younger group of boys, 25 per cent have good or fair, 65 per cent poor, and 10 per cent vicious recreations.

It is important for the probation officer to know not only what recreations are characteristic of the group of delinquents but also the effect of one type of amusement on the total recreational picture. It has often been assumed that developing some constructive interest considerably modifies or terminates undesirable activities; whereas all poor and vicious pastimes are closely related. To test the truth of these assertions, club membership, reading, movie attendance, sports, street life, and sex activities are analyzed in relation to the individual's total recreation classification.

Club Membership. The term "club" is used here to designate an organization sponsored by a reputable civic or social agency and directed by a "leader," who is presumably older and more experienced than the "members." The club meets regularly, has rules and a definite program. This type of organization should not be confused with the ordinary street gang that is self-organized and self-governed and that lacks the inspiration and direction of a club leader.

Approximately one-third of the group (33 per cent of the boys and 28 per cent of the girls) are enrolled in clubs.

Since no controls were used in this study, it is impossible to state the percentage of delinquents among club members as compared with non-club members. However, it is certainly true that club membership does not suffice to keep the individual from supplementary, low-grade recreations. Of the young people having poor recreations, one-fifth were club members, and of those having vicious recreations, a quarter were club members.

It is true, however, that while club membership is not incompatible with low-grade recreations, it still does help to raise the general leisure time status. Among the boys, club membership is found in conjunction with other good recreations three times as frequently as with poor; among the girls, five times as frequently. More than half of the young people (58 per cent of the boys and 50 per cent of the girls) reporting good recreations are club members.

Some relation can be traced between the general recreation rating and the type of club. The tendency is for girls with otherwise vicious pastimes to belong to social clubs only; that is, clubs for dancing, parties, and cards; while those with good recreations belong to Girl Reserves or settlement house clubs for music, sewing, cooking, dramatics, and reading.[4] Girls belonging to clubs organized for indoor games, hikes, and sports are distributed equally among the Good, Fair, Poor and Vicious. No such clear-cut division exists among the boys. The fourteen Boy Scouts, for example, are classified as follows: Good, two; Fair, four; Poor, six; and Vicious, two. Only boys

---

[4] Since in many instances the activities of the clubs were not specifically stated, these figures are not conclusive.

reported Good belong to clubs organized for aircraft, wood-carving, carpentry, and clay modeling. All other types of clubs appear to more or less degree in all categories.

Club membership bears no significant correlation with age. Yet the excess of membership among the older girls as compared with the lack among older boys suggests that clubs organized along present lines may be more efficacious in satisfying the needs of the adolescent girl than of the adolescent boy.

Reading. Reading is reported as a prominent interest of 187 boys and 41 girls. Contrasted with them are twenty-two boys and seven girls who state either that they definitely dislike reading or simply that they never read anything. All of the remainder, if pressed, would admit some reading, good or bad; but few could name any books or stories that particularly interested them.

"Good reading" is reported for ninety-seven boys and seventeen girls. This classification, taken over from the Judge Baker Foundation Summary, is derived from such statements as "Reads Literary Digest, books of travel and other good literature." "Fair reading" is recorded for fifty-seven boys and eleven girls. An examination of these records shows a mixture of questionable or even undesirable material, such as "Western stories" and other thrillers, cheaply written, and some of the books always found on approved reading lists. "Fair" implies a balance of good and poor reading as well as material difficult to classify as either. The reading of thirty-three boys and thirteen girls is described as "poor," "cheap," or "trashy," consisting entirely of such things as confession magazines, gangster stories, vulgar joke books, and tabloid newspapers.

The readers of good literature among the boys fall into the different recreation groups as follows: Good, 31 per cent; Fair, 35 per cent; Poor, 31 per cent; and Vicious, 3 per cent. The distribution among the girls is quite different: Good, 59 per cent; Fair, 30 per cent; Poor, none; and Vicious, 11 per cent. That is, there is greater likelihood that the girl with good recreations will read good books than will the boy with good recreations.

In the good recreation group there are twenty-five boys reading good literature to one reading poor, while among the girls the proportion is still greater, sixty-five to none. In the vicious recreation group there is only one boy reading good literature to four reading poor, and one girl to two.

In visiting the settlements, churches, club houses and schools in which the various clubs to which these children belonged held their meetings, the writer noted almost invariably that the organizations possessed books that were kept either in the club rooms themselves or in a library to which all club members had access. Club leaders frequently mentioned their efforts to instill in their members a love of reading. The findings of this study indicate that their efforts were successful. Seventy per cent of the boys who read good material are club members as compared with only 40 per cent of those whose reading is fair and 15 per cent of those whose reading material is poor. The percentages among the girls are 35, 28, and 15 respectively.[5]

If approached from the point of view of club membership the relation is similarly signficant. Of 130 boys who are club members 72 (55 per cent) are rated as having good reading, while only 12 per cent of the persons not belonging to clubs received this grade.

Movies. Slightly more than one-half of the 500 children expressed an interest in movies (219 boys and 47 girls). Of these, 190 boys and 30 girls reported moderate attendance and enjoyment. Boys and girls show no significant difference in regularity of attendance, the occasions for each ranging from once a month to two or three times a week. What is more surprising, for only twenty boys and seven girls was movie

[5] During the course of this investigation the writer interviewed the club leaders in the following settlement houses and recreation centers: Elizabeth Peabody House, South End House and South Bay Union, Little House, Dennison House, Lincoln House, North Bennett Industrial School, Roxbury Neighborhood House, Willard Settlement, Bunker Hill Boys' Club, Morgan Memorial, Young Men's Christian Association, and North End Catholic Guild. In most cases a list of the children claiming to be members of clubs was sent in advance to each institution. The aim of a conference with the club leaders was to get information on the following topics as related to each child: dates of membership, activities engaged in, attendance, attitude toward the club leader, attitude toward companions, personality assets and liabilities, and the leader's impressions regarding the effect of probation on the child.

attendance considered excessive; all of these went to the movies four or more times per week. Several of the boys went every night and two or three times day times, as well, frequently stealing the admission money, gaining entrance by evading the ticket collectors, or sneaking in via emergency exits. Some boys and girls habitually made movie houses places of refuge to escape truant officers and irate parents. Seven boys and nine girls stated they had never seen a movie, but all were eager for the opportunity.

Movie attendance bears no significant relation to the recreation classification, except that the small groups who attend movies excessively all fall under the category Poor or Vicious recreation. Movie attendance likewise bears no relationship to club membership, except that few club members are found among excessive movie goers.

Sports. Sports, outdoor and gymnasium activities, and games are divided on the basis of type into "team sports" and "non-team sports." The former includes baseball, basketball, hockey, and all sports demanding organized teams or sides who must play together; the latter includes hiking, fishing, swimming, and other activities not demanding a definite number, or organization. Not one of the 100 girls plays or has any interest in playing team sports. Seventy-five boys belong to football, baseball, or basketball teams. Some teams are self-organized teams that practice on vacant lots and public playgrounds; others are organized and are coached by professional leaders, and play regularly in gymnasiums loaned or rented to them by settlements, club houses and recreation centers. Non-team sports are listed for 119 boys and 15 girls. Neither type of activity bears any relation to recreation classification, club membership, or age. The difference in the proportion of boys and girls, however, is noteworthy.

Street Life. "Street life" is equivalent to the expression "turned loose on the streets." It means, in its mildest form, undirected play in the middle of the street or in an alley, restricted only by "Don'ts" screamed from a fourth or fifth floor window, or by a policeman's club. In its worst form it means loafing, aimless wandering, hopping automobiles, or group activity ranging from wrestling or throwing stones to organized street theft and "fishing drunks." Since almost every child reporting "street life" as recreation lives in congested, if not unhygienic, and disreputable districts, the term implies contact with the lowest type of environmental influences. In many cases, the mere fact of playing on the street near home means exposure to profane and obscene language, drunkenness, carousing, vice, and even fights and brawls.

"Street life" in this sense is listed as an important use of leisure time by 41 per cent of the boys and by 22 per cent of the girls. That is, two-fifths of all the boys find a large part of their amusement on the street instead of with books, in taking part in sports or games, in walking or talking with parents or friends, or in any other type of approved activity. The number of girls is not so large. Girls being more closely guarded report that they "stay in the house" or "sit on the doorstep." One mother boasted "my girl don't run around on the street; she helps me with the work or sits right there in that chair all day long." The girls who report street life are largely those who have escaped from parental control. Fourteen of the twenty-two wander on the streets at night.

Closely allied to street life are two other groups of activities. The first group includes gambling by means of cards, dice, or roulette, excessive attendance at public dance halls and beach gaming stands, loafing, "joy-riding," "bunking," and drinking.[6] Participation in these pursuits is listed eighty-six times for sixty-four boys and forty-five times for twenty-six girls. Obviously the majority of both boys and girls with these recreations are classified as Vicious, though not one of the activities is restricted entirely to this category. Bunking, for example, was reported for one boy whose recreation during the day was very good and whose general classification was "Fair."

[6] "Joy-riding" is a term used by the children themselves meaning automobile rides of boys and girls at night unchaperoned. Every case included here presented some irregularity of conduct—girls going against their parents' wishes, boys drinking, or stealing cars in which to ride. "Bunking" means sleeping in some place away from home, usually on roofs, in shacks, in alleys or doorways, in parks, or in public buildings.

Only 27 per cent of the boys and 22 per cent of the girls represented here were club members.

Sex Activities. In effect, several of the activities listed above are closely allied to the next category which for lack of a better term, is called "sex play." Joy-riding with subsequent "petting," as well as loafing and bunking are frequently stepping stones to immorality and sex perversions. Sex activity, including masturbation,[7] sexual intercourse, and various forms of perversion, is reported by seventy-five boys and twenty-nine girls, or one-fifth of the entire group. Ordinarily these activities do not find a place in a catalogue of recreations, but since they are reported by so many children as their major or only pleasure they cannot be ignored.[8]

Of the seventy-six boys about one-half (52 per cent) belong to gangs organized solely for sex play or including it in their activities. Sometimes they attack small girls or invite them to their rendezvous to join in their sports. They belong usually to the lower and middle age group. The remaining 48 per cent include chiefly older boys who frequent houses of prostitution, or who repeatedly commit sex acts with girls; and both younger and older boys who consort with homosexuals.

Of the twenty-nine girls, twenty-one commit sex acts regularly, three being professional street walkers. The remaining eight have incestuous relations with fathers or brothers or engage in mutual masturbation with sisters.

Only 21 per cent of these boys and 22 per cent of the girls are club members.

PROBATION TREATMENT

The preceding pages have shown that the search for diversion or entertainment or "a thrill" often leads youth into patterns of behavior known as delinquency. In considering the recreations of the group in relation to treatment, the probation

---

[7] "Masturbation" here refers to mutual masturbation only, as the information on self-masturbation showed such lack of uniformity as to make it unreliable for statistical purposes.

[8] Readers of *The Polish Peasant* by Thomas and Znaniecki will recall in the autobiography of the peasant boy, Wladek Wiszniewski, how frequently he refers to leisure spent in "foolishing" with girls.

officer has to solve for each individual the problems of how far the individual's leisure time interests have caused or contributed to his delinquency and what can best be done for him. The Clinic estimates of recreational activities as causative or contributing factors in the delinquency and the recommendations in each case supply a basis for treatment.

Leisure time interests are listed as contributing to delinquency 133 times among the 400 boys (33 per cent) and 18 times among the 100 girls (18 per cent). In 103 cases (78 per cent) of the former, excessive street life was held responsible and of them 33 reported no other interests whatever. In thirty cases, street life was accompanied by gambling, loafing with a bad gang, or frequenting disreputable houses. For fourteen of the eighteen girls (78 per cent) excessive night life on the streets and beaches was listed as leading to delinquency. The remaining four were referred to as "lacking proper recreational outlets."

The evidence presented above is sufficient to establish the fact that there exists a definite relationship between poor types of recreation (whether due to individual choice or to lack of recreational facilities) and delinquency.

The following list showing the relation between parental control and recreation rating suggests that delinquency is the end of a sequence which begins with lack of parental oversight and guidance, followed by undesirable recreation and bad companions.

	PERCENTAGE WITH POOR PARENTAL CONTROL	
RECREATION	BOYS	GIRLS
Good	21	13
Fair....................	32	43
Poor	35	47
Vicious	62	95

Only a small percentage of children whose recreation is classified as good show any lack of parental control or supervision. But the numbers gradually increase as recreation becomes poorer. Only 5 per cent of girls rated vicious have any normal parental control. The extremes of both series show significant differences.

For 163 boys (41 per cent) and 34 girls (34 per cent), the Clinic specifically advised that attention be given to problems of recreation. Recommendations for improvement are not restricted to the children whose pastimes were classified as poor or vicious. For example, a boy whose recreation is normal during the school year may need a camp during the summer. For the delicate child, out-of-door play should perhaps be substituted for indoor games and music. Suggestions of this type have been included as well as the more frequent statements: "Link boy up with some good club" or "Girl needs facilities for recreation."

PERCENTAGE FOR WHOM
RECOMMENDATIONS WERE MADE

RECREATION	BOYS	GIRLS
Good	28	0
Fair	30	30
Poor	52	53
Vicious	43	35

If recreation is poor why are there not always recommendations that something be done? The answer lies in the fact that other recommendations are sometimes made that indirectly affect leisure habits. Suggestions treated under the headings "Companionship" and "Place of Living" are especially pertinent. In every case where recreation was listed as a "causation" there was either a recommendation for improvement of recreation, or a more drastic suggestion such as commitment to a reform institution, foster home placement, case work with the family, or moving. In many cases a change regarding companionship was designated to alter the recreation situation, especially in the younger age group. For older children "work" requirements took precedence, especially for boys who spent much time loafing.

Methods used by the Probation Officer. Did the probation officer fulfill the recreation recommendations? If so, what methods did he use? If not, why did he fail to do so? What effect does change of recreation have upon change of conduct?

Of 163 recommendations for boys, 80 (48 per cent) were fulfilled, 24 (14.5 per cent) were attempted, 59 (36.5 per cent) show no record of anything having been done; of the 34 recommendations for girls, 16 (42 per cent) were fulfilled, 8 (23 per cent) were attempted, and 10 (29 per cent) were not attempted.

Only about one-third of the recommendations were specific as "Try to interest Mrs. C. of —— Settlement House in Anna and give her an opportunity to develop new interests." In every instance among the girls and in 90 per cent of the cases among the boys these specific suggestions were followed. The advantage of understanding neighborhood facilities and persons connected with them cannot be overemphasized. For many years the Directors of the Clinic have known intimately the personnel of recreational institutions. For example, the Judge Baker Foundation advised that the probation officers consult "Mr. K." with regard to the problems of twelve boys. In every case the suggestion was followed. Mr. K. in every case enrolled the boy in a club; but more than that, he established a permanent contact. Every boy became a respectful and admiring friend and follower. Social engineering demands not only knowledge of social resources, but a penetrating insight into their use for solving individual problems.

In no type of treatment has the probation officer shown more enthusiasm and more persistence (and less good judgment) than in dealing with recreation. Organized clubs have come in for the lion's share of attention. Of the 179 boys for whom some recreational reform was attempted, 96 (53 per cent) were advised or urged to attend clubs. Of these, 81 (84 per cent) became regular members. When this number is added to the number of boys already club members and not heretofore included in this section, it raises the total to 211 who at some time belonged to organized clubs. Of these 162 (40 per cent of 400) were considered active club members at the time their cases were filed.

The recommendation "Get the boy linked up with some club" means more than getting his name enrolled on a club roster. It means more from the point of view of social engineering than the probation officer's casually remarking over his shoulder, "Why don't you join Mr. B.'s class in airplane construction?" or seriously saying with a stern look in his eye, "Look here, I don't want to see you on the street. You must join one of the clubs at —— Settlement House." It means a subtle suggestion and skillful maneuvering—arranging that Tony shall report at a settlement house just at the time when exciting clubs are meeting, introducing Tony to leaders by taking him on car rides or on hikes with them, giving him tickets to games or club entertainments. The establishment of rapport between boy and club is facilitated or prevented by the time, place, and conditions of the first approach.

One probation officer tells of her experiences with two girls when taken to the same settlement house. Sophia had never had any playmates of her own age; but was kept closely at home with her invalid mother, a scowling, abusive grandmother, and four younger brothers. She had never been allowed to play with other children, but had spent many hours working on lovely Lithuanian embroidery which her mother had taught her. Sophia was teased at school because of her shy manner and scolded at home because she did not progress as rapidly as her younger brothers. Lacking the diversions which she saw others enjoying, Sophia resorted to day dreaming. Contact with girls by means of clubs was recommended. Before making any suggestions to Sophia or her parents, Miss B. consulted the girls' directors of three recreation centers. At last she discovered a small club of girls near Sophia's age who had been organized to "draw and paint," but as none were really artistic, interest was waning. Miss B. suggested that Sophia be asked to join the club in order to teach the other girls to embroider. The solution was a happy one. Sophia entered with the feeling that she was welcomed, even sought. Her friendship with two of the girls has continued over the five years which have elapsed.

Miss B. was not so successful in her treatment of Mary.

Soon after Mary's arrest and clinical examination Miss B. learned that a very good club leader at the same settlement was organizing a small dramatic club. The probation officer was very anxious for Mary to join as she had discovered that she not only was interested, but had considerable talent along this line. She hurriedly went to fetch her since this was the last day of registration. When they entered the room, one of the girls turned aside with a sneer and said, "She's a crook. Let's not have any crooks in our plays." Mary was so humiliated that she would never again consider for a moment joining any club or taking a part in a play.

During their probation, arrangements were made for fifty-five boys to be sent out of the city on vacations, but in seven cases parents were not willing. Of the forty-eight who did go, twelve were in caddy camps and twenty in camps run by social agencies, Salvation Army, and men's civic clubs. The remaining sixteen were sent to a special farm, or to friends or relatives of the children's parents or of the probation officer.

The next largest group of activities initiated by the probation officer comprised swimming, skating, and hiking. For thirteen boys these sports were substituted for street life.

Some form of art, woodcarving, clay modeling, drawing or painting, and music became new interests for eight boys. Seven other boys were introduced to new diversions by probation officers: two were taught to rear and train pigeons for racing, two to ride bicycles, and three to play other games such as chess and checkers. In addition to the above, which were all activities extending over considerable periods of time, countless outings and pleasures of shorter duration were enjoyed by children on probation. Free tickets for boat and bus excursions, picnics, amusement parks, carnivals, ball games, circuses, movies, and amateur dramatic performances, were given— sometimes as rewards for good records, sometimes not.

One probation officer skillfully uses his trips to visit out-of-town charges for several purposes. Instead of going alone he fills his automobile with boys who he knows enjoy riding in the country or who are in danger of getting into mischief on the street. Sometimes he plans that a probationer shall by this means meet other boys whose influence promises to be good. Often the purpose is only to get better acquainted with the boys, to break down their reserve, or to observe them in their relations with their companions. Sometimes he takes only one child in order to discuss with him privately and at leisure problems arising in the home situation or personal conflicts.

In a district having no parks or playgrounds a probation officer persuaded the owner of a vacant lot to allow boys to use it for a football field. Another officer created recreation facilities by having his probationers convert a wet, smelly alley into a neighborhood play center. A local blacksmith contributed horseshoes and a quoits contest was launched. Fathers and older boys of the neighborhood became interested and soon "Horseshoe Alley" was a center of attraction.

Three of the probation officers told the writer of their frequent appearances before city councils and civic and social agencies of various kinds to plead for additional playgrounds and better playground equipment and supervision, and to try to bring before the attention of local groups the seriousness of the amusement problem.

Throughout the entire analysis of recreation treatment a difference is apparent between those persons whose recreation is poor because of lack of facilities and those who choose poor recreations when more desirable ones are available. Probation is far more effective in prevention than in reform. To "develop good interests" where there are none is easier than "to substitute good interests for poor." For example, providing diversion for Fred Maxwell required the most persistent efforts of his probation officer for a period of four months.

Fred had been in court for forgery. He desired more than anything to be popular with a gang of young crooks on his street. In order to ingratiate himself he had stolen money for treats. Though only sixteen years old, Fred had much of the attitude of a hardened criminal. The probation officer tried to interest him in various activities at a settlement house. Fred refused to attend. The probation officer invited him to go on hikes and rides. Fred declined. All of his leisure was spent with the gang. Finally the probation officer threatened to send him to a state training school, but he could not be sure Fred was obeying unless he had his eye on him, consequently he ate his own dinner early, went to Fred's house, took him by the arm and marched him over to the Y.M.C.A. swimming pool. Evening after evening the probation officer swam with Fred teaching him new strokes, pitting him against other boys and encouraging him to enter contests. Unless the probation officer conducted Fred personally, he did not go. Four months later Fred won first prize in a Y contest and was invited to spend the week-end in the country with a young man who won second prize. The probation officer helped Fred prepare for the trip and instructed him in the etiquette and social customs involved. When he returned, Fred came to the probation officer's room to tell him that he was through with the gang and crooking; for he had found there were more worth-while people to know and more satisfactory things to do. He was soon promoted to a position of some responsibility. He has continued his swimming and has made a record for obstacle swimming in rapid streams.

All probation officers find "Recreation" an agreeable topic with which to open conversation with parents. It is much easier to ask a mother "How does Lizzie spend her free time?" than "Does Lizzie still steal money from you?" This topic ranks next to "Health" as an opening wedge for further contact with parents. No topic is more useful as the basis for parent-child understanding where family relationships are not ideal. In a few cases parents are urged by probation officers to allow their children more freedom. In most cases, parents are advised to show more interest and to give better supervision to their children at play. Instead of chasing the children out of the house with a warning, "Now, don't come back in till noon," mothers are warned of the bad influences to be encountered on the street and are urged to take all the children to the park for the afternoon. In all cases the officer emphasizes the necessity for parents' knowing where and how their children are playing and suggests means of recreation in which the whole family may take part. In helping the family to budget their expenses the probation officer mentions recreation and suggests the buying of a few simple toys or musical instruments or laying aside money for entertainments, outings, and other pleasures. An especially disastrous point of view is often encountered, namely, that it is the business of parents to see that their children are clothed, fed, and sent to school, but that they should be free to play as they please. Other members of the family, older brothers and sisters, and relatives are encouraged to feel a responsibility for supervision of the leisure time activities of the young delinquent and are urged to try deliberately to help steer the recalcitrant child into better diversions.

Why Recreation Recommendations were not Fulfilled. Failure to enlist children in constructive use of leisure is due both to limitations of the environment and to inadequate technique. As implied in an earlier section, many times the recommendations were general rather than specific. This is true either because facilities were lacking, or were inadequately known; or because the probation officer was supposed to know or find them. For example, "Try to improve Harry's use of leisure time" was a challenge to the probation officer to find outlets.

On more than one occasion club leaders refused admission to children with reputations for quarreling, rowdyism, profanity, or delinquency. One settlement house director said frankly, "We have enough difficulty quelling the spontaneous deviltry of our regular club members. We see no reason for aggravating it by admitting other persons who have a record of misbehavior."

In at least thirty-seven cases (thirty-two boys and five girls) where "No attempts to improve recreation" is assumed, other more drastic treatment, such as moving, finding a job, or foster home placement, has been used. Recreation needs are disregarded until other more urgent needs are met.

In their enthusiasm to arrange "suitable" programs for children, probation officers have apparently failed in many cases to appreciate the importance of the child's enjoyment. Officers have tended to consider baseball, tennis, cooking, dramatics, and reading as desirable without first determining whether the children upon whom they are imposed derive satisfaction from them. No pastime is enjoyable unless it is successful. The child with low mentality or with poor muscular coördination cannot indefinitely "enjoy" a competitive sport in which he does not have the satisfaction that comes from winning. Play ideals sink lower and lower until they reach a level where success is attainable. If this does not happen, there is conflict between ideal and practice.

In no instance was the probation officer successful in improving the recreation of a child of "abnormal personality." The task of developing for these children desirable reactions while engaged in play required more time and persistent effort than the probation officer was able to give. Club leaders were likewise unsuccessful. Other persons who could not be interested were street habitués and children with low mentality. There is no evidence that either boys or girls who have been accustomed to burlesque shows, petting parties, or gang life on the street can be induced by the probation officer to abandon these forms of recreation and leave the bright lights to take up more subdued pastimes at home or in clubs supervised by social workers.

RECREATION AND OUTCOME

What has been the effect on behavior of attempts to improve recreation? Does the boy who joins a club stop stealing? In short, does recreation affect the character and morals of a delinquent, or does it affect only his happiness and his superficial attitudes?

Good recreational interests act as a safeguard, poor or deficient pleasures act as a menace. These facts are substantiated by the relation between outcome and by changes in recreation while on probation.

The previous recreation of the delinquent is one of the best prognoses. Table XXXIII in the Appendix shows that the percentage of success is twice as great for the boy or girl whose previous recreation was rated Good as for those whose recreation was Vicious. The percentage of temporary success is approximately the same for all recreation groups, but the proportion of failure is much greater for Vicious than for Good

(36 per cent to 7 per cent for boys and 38 per cent to none for girls).

The probation officer is more successful in preventing further delinquency by providing adequate recreation for the boy or girl who has none, than he is in reforming existing undesirable behavior patterns. Boys and girls spending their leisure in street life, joy-riding, loafing, drinking, gambling, and in sex activities were in many cases prohibited by the probation officer from these activities but seldom did the mere fact of eliminating these recreations improve conduct. Recreational life cannot really be said to be improved until constructive pastimes are substituted for the old and until new associations and social attitudes have been built up. Although less than one-half of all the Clinic's suggestions were carried out, improvements in recreation were made for more than one-third of the group. Through the efforts of the probation officer eighty-one boys and fifteen girls became active members of clubs (a few had belonged to clubs previously but had dropped out). Of these, all the girls and 70 per cent of the boys were successes. This type of treatment was more efficacious than sending the young people away on vacations. Of the forty-eight boys who went away from home for all or a part of their vacations 66 per cent were successes. Often boys were sent to camps or to the country to separate them from bad companions.

Success in eliminating undesirable recreation habits depends upon three things: (1) coöperation of the parents and other members of the family in the matter of supervision, and in planning recreations in the home; (2) solving problems of companionships; (3) providing facilities and leadership. A significant contrast is found between two selected groups. Group A is composed of seven boys and girls who did not have any parental supervision and who continued their vicious recreations in spite of the probation officer's efforts. All were failures. Group B is composed of sixteen boys and girls who had good parental control and who responded to the suggestions made by the probation officer regarding recreation and companionship. Of these, twelve have no further record of delinquency to date and the remaining three abstained from misbehavior for more than two years. The delinquency of the younger offender is often related to his leisure time activities and the type of companions he has, hence improvement in associates and in recreation usually eliminates delinquent behavior. But for the older delinquent the connection is less evident and the outcome less certain.

SUMMARY AND CONCLUSIONS

Constructive leisure time interests of delinquent children are extremely meager and facilities for desirable recreation are limited. Only one out of every six has an adequate recreational program, while almost one-fifth of the delinquents engage in pastimes prohibited by law. Using the categories, Good, Fair, Poor, and Vicious to rate the recreation of delinquents previous to probation, the modal group for boys is Poor, while for girls it is Fair. A larger percentage of girls than boys are rated Vicious. Ten per cent of the younger children engage in Vicious recreations as compared with 20 per cent of the older.

Poor recreation or lack of recreational facilities is listed as contributing to the delinquency of one out of three offenders. Many have also "poor parental control and supervision" or "bad companions" listed as probable causations. It seems evident therefore that in many cases parental coöperation must be enlisted and bad companions eliminated before a constructive recreation program can be worked out. Good interests such as clubs and sports do not preclude poor pastimes, nor does the prohibiting of poor recreations lead automatically to the adoption of desirable pastimes.

The probation officer attempted to improve the recreation of more then one-half of the total group, and was successful in two cases out of three. The forms of recreation promoted by the officer include: club activities, vacation trips, outdoor sports—both team and non-team sports—games, and reading. Free tickets, picnics, trips, and entertainments served to establish rapport. Pastimes which the officer tried to eliminate include: "street life," excessive movie attendance, "poor reading," loafing, bunking, "joy-riding," drinking, sex play, and gambling.

Probation is more successful in developing good recreations where the child has no interests than in substituting good interests for poor. It is especially difficult to provide constructive amusements sufficiently exciting to appeal to the young man or woman who has been engaging in "joy-riding," "crooking," and illicit sex activities. Probation officers seem in some cases to have defeated their own purposes by insisting upon types of recreation considered by them "good" without judging the value of the activity by the extent to which it satisfies the needs of the child. The failure to carry out recreation recommendations, though due largely to lack of facilities, was often attributable to the unwillingness or inability of settlements and clubs to enroll delinquents. It seems ironic that social agencies founded and supported on the assumption that their recreational programs are valuable socializing agencies should refuse admission to those individuals who need them most.

The success or failure of the delinquent is largely determined by his leisure-time habits. Both boys and girls whose recreation prior to probation was rated Good showed twice as large a percentage of success-to-date as those whose recreation was rated Vicious. Conversely, the proportion of failure was five or more times as great. This means that, in spite of the efforts of the probation officer, delinquents who have developed undesirable recreation habits are less likely to be successes. The results of probation treatment are equally conclusive. Among delinquents who followed the officers' recreation suggestions the percentage of success is twice as high as among those who did not. Among both boys and girls probation treatment of recreation was more successful for the younger group than for the older.

These findings indicate first, an urgent need on the part of the community to provide ample recreation resources which will be available to all; and second, the desirability of more skilled technique on the part of probation officers in fitting the recreation to the needs of the individual child.

CHAPTER VII

Probation and Work

Broadly speaking "work" means the performance of useful tasks and may be applied to the daily needs of the home, such as sweeping, carrying coal, running errands, and tending children, as well as to "gainful employment" outside of the home. Because of the difficulty of securing adequate information about the former, this study deals only with the latter type of activity.

What kind of jobs do delinquent children hold? Do their jobs expose them to degrading influences, or does employment tend to keep children out of mischief? What is the relation between unemployment and delinquency? Does a court record limit a child's chances of employment? Can the probation officer assist the child in finding work or prevent unsuitable employment? Can the probation officer force the lazy child to work? Is there a relation between whether or not a child is employed and his success on probation? These are questions which this study seeks to answer.

THE WORK RECORD OF THE DELINQUENT

One-half of these young people, when they were first known to the probation officer, had already been engaged in gainful employment. To them "work" was not a thing to dream of for the future, but a reality of the present. The percentage of girls working was almost as great as of boys, and the percentage of girls holding full-time jobs was larger than for boys. (See Table XIII.)

Those who have held or are holding part-time or temporary jobs are chiefly school children who work after school, or on

TABLE XIII

*The work experience of 500 delinquent children at time
of the Judge Baker Foundation examination*

	Boys		Girls		Total	
	Num-ber	Per cent	Num-ber	Per cent	Num-ber	Per cent
Had never been gainfully employed....	210	53	61	61	271	54
Had held or were holding part time or temporary jobs	109	27	12	12	121	24
Had held or were holding full-time jobs..	81	20	27	27	108	22
Total...........................	400	100	100	100	500	100

Saturdays and in vacations; they are mostly boys. They include the newsboys, bootblacks, and errand-running youngsters who are seen darting here and there in the busy streets of the city. They are also boys sent to farms and camps for all or part of their vacations, who in return for board and lodging work at whatever tasks are assigned them. In a few cases they earn wages in addition to board and room. But since they have not agreed to any specific hours and are not bound by any very definite requirements, their position is not comparable to that of a "farm hand" employed by contract.

The opportunities for girls to earn spending money by part-time employment are limited. The only two activities reported for as many as two persons are tending neighbors' children (five) and street selling (three).

The third group contains the full-time wage earners, the young people who have "put away childish things" and have "gone to work." It comprises largely boys and girls in factories, stores, offices, and shops. It is highly significant that of these 108 children who had left school and sought employment only seven (six boys and one girl) could be classified as having "adequate vocational adjustment." This term is used to describe a person who is normally happy in a job suitable to his or her capabilities, and providing opportunity for advancement in proportion to growth and maturity. The majority of the children are in "blind alley" jobs, with no plan for the future. Even of the boys in skilled trades such as printing, painting, dairying, laundry, and automobile repairing, less than 10 per cent are receiving any training. That is, they are not apprentices but unskilled laborers.

TABLE XIV

Work record of 229 delinquents

Positions held by 190 boys prior to Judge Baker Foundation examination*

Errand boy	42
Factory worker (shoe, candy, necktie, box, paper, and clothing factories)	29
Store employees (probably includes delivery boy)	29
Shining shoes	26
Newsboy	25
Peddler or peddler's helper	20
Driver's helper for the delivery of ice, milk, and laundry	17
Caddy	12
Western Union messenger	11
Farm helper	10
Garage worker	9
Driver of team, Office boy (5 each)	10
Waterboy	4
Printer's helper, Bowling alley—"pin boy" (3 each)	6
Laundry worker, Guide for blind men (2 each)	4
Hotel—dishwasher, "bell-hop" (2 each)	4
Baker's helper, Dairy, Potter, Hospital attendant, Cleaner, Painter (1 each)	6
Total	264

Positions held by 39 girls

Factory worker	17
Domestic servant (maid, waitress)	6
Mother's helper (tending children)	5
Office girl (typist, filing clerk, cashier, errand girl)	4
Peddler	3
Salesgirl (five-and-ten cent store)	2
Artist's model	1
Farmer's helper (pulling radishes)	1
Total	39

* The purpose of this list is to show the kinds of work done by delinquent boys. Therefore it includes all jobs held in the past instead of only the ones in operation at the time of examination.

The most depressing features of the employment of "underprivileged children" as revealed by investigation of the jobs

shown in Table XIV are: tendency of employers to exploit
minors, the child's inability to improve his occupational status,
and the lack of planning for the future.

Very few of the full-time or part-time workers were guided
in their employment by either personal choice or the advice
of vocational guidance experts. The necessity of earning money
forced most of them to accept any opportunity available.

RELATION BETWEEN EMPLOYMENT AND DELINQUENCY

The probation officer must, of course, be acquainted with
the work history of his charges but he is primarily concerned
with their employment or unemployment as it is related to
their delinquency.

Sixty-five children (forty-six boys and nineteen girls) presented unemployment problems at the time they were taken
for study. "Unemployment" is used to mean "not having a
job" and implies that work is desired. The term applies to
four boys and four girls who have never been employed,
but who are qualified to work and who want work, as well
as to forty-two boys and fifteen girls who are temporarily
idle. Either the delinquents themselves are seeking jobs or
their parents are seeking jobs for them. There is not always
agreement between them. Refusing to work is the basic reason
for twelve parents' filing charges of stubbornness against their
children. One boy ran away to escape the heavy drudgery of
his father's bakery shop. Two boys and two girls ran away or
bunked out because they could not find employment and did
not dare face their scolding parents. On the other hand, there
are some children whose keen desire to find a position is opposed by fond parents who wish to keep their children dependent upon them. This condition arises where parents, and
especially mothers, try to keep their children from growing up.
One mother who feared her own approaching age tried to keep
young by pretending that "her sons" were "little children."
Two other mothers attempted to buy their sons' affection by
means of large sums of spending money, and opposed their
earning money on the outside.

In nine instances among the boys and in three among the girls unemployment resulted from apprehension in delinquency. Four boys lost their positions as a result of attempts to steal from their employers, two by taking merchandise, one by forgery and the other by keeping a pay envelope given him by mistake. Three boys ran away from home giving up good places to accompany "crooks," who offered to teach them to make money more easily by illegal means. One boy who worked on a milk wagon was urged by his foster parents to supply them with milk. When this was discovered, he was dismissed. Two boys made money by stealing chickens from the market and selling them to a restaurant keeper, who suggested the plan to them. Their jobs ended when their employer was put in jail.

In the case of the girls it is very difficult to distinguish between cause and effect. Of the fifteen unemployed girls nine were apprehended for sex offenses, or brought to court on "wayward" or "stubborn" complaints. It is difficult to tell whether bad conduct caused the girls to be "fired" or whether they gave up their jobs because they sought an easier life. Three girls who were prostitutes defended their profession saying they saw no reason for working eight hours a day for $10.00 a week when they could earn five times as much in a few hours a day.

Low wages was given as an excuse for shoplifting by seven girls. No girl in this study earned more than $12.00 per week, while the median wage of full-time workers was $9.50 per week.

PROBATION TREATMENT

The probation officer has to take into account two different attitudes toward work. The children and often their parents are interested in the immediate financial returns, while he is concerned primarily in steering children into places that will satisfy their individual needs and will enable them to become useful citizens. Although he wishes to take a long-time view, he cannot disregard the emergency aspect of the problems presented. In fact, plans for the future can often be introduced only by gaining confidence through solving the problems of the present.

For exactly one hundred children the Clinic made recommendations regarding work. These recommendations fall into three major groups: the first concerns getting jobs for the unemployed; the second, vocational adjustment of children having part- or full-time work; the third, that certain persons should stop work. The accompanying summary reveals the types of recommendations.

For one out of ten of the whole group, immediate employment was suggested. Recommendations for work are much more frequently made for boys than for girls. The situations briefly sketched below illustrate the three types of problems with all of which the probation officer must deal.

Illustration of Recommendations for Immediate Employment.

John B. is sixteen years old and is repeating the eighth grade. He dislikes school, so truants frequently. He is the oldest of a family of nine children. His father is a day laborer, hard working, sober, and affectionate, but he has recently developed tuberculosis. Since John's intelligence quotient is low and he is not likely to benefit greatly by additional schooling, he is advised to stop school and go to work to help support the family.

Bertrand L. had appropriated an automobile, collided with a telephone pole, and remonstrated with an officer for taking him to court. For five years he had been periodically getting into trouble. He had killed a neighbor's dog, stolen a box containing $18.00 of Red Cross money from his schoolteacher, and had stolen various other things from relatives and neighbors. Each time his father had made restitution and Bertrand had only been required to apologize. The Clinic urged that the father require Bertrand to go to work and earn the money to pay for damages on the car.

Esther M., age sixteen, has always been industrious and obedient, although she has inwardly felt very unhappy because her parents will not allow her to get a job. Her friends all work and have money to spend for cosmetics, silk hose, and accessories. She longs for the same things but knows that she will be scolded if she begs her parents for them. After she was caught for shoplifting in Filene's

Basement, the Clinic recommended that the probation officer persuade the parents to allow Esther to work, and help her to find employment suitable to her limited capacities.

TABLE XV

Judge Baker Foundation recommendations regarding work

Type of Recommendation	Number		
	Boys	Girls	Total
Immediate employment	*46*	*6*	*52*
Type not specified.........................	25	2	27
Type specified............................	21	4	25
Vocational adjustment	*26*	*6*	*32*
Change from part-time to full-time work......	4	0	4
Change to different type....................	16	6	22
Adjustment of hours, wages, or attitude toward work....................................	6	0	6
Stop work	*3*	*13*	*16*
To return to school	1	2	3
Because unlawfully employed................	2	0	2
To assist with housework in own home........	0	5	5
To assist with housework in boarding house....	0	6	6
Total...................................	75	25	100

In almost one-half these cases there is added to the injunction, "Get a job," advice regarding the particular types of work for which the child is best fitted. This is usually determined by special vocational testing. Not only is it necessary that he (or she) be working so as to be kept out of mischief, or to earn needed money, or to get the discipline of a strong employer; but it is also essential that this activity shall be of the kind to give satisfactions. Some of the specific types of employment suggested by the Clinic are: (1) apprenticeship or work as helper in keeping with discovered special abilities; (2) farm work to insure exercise in the open air; (3) routine work for persons of limited intelligence; (4) sedentary work or work not requiring great physical activity or strength for physically handicapped persons; (5) work in another locality to separate the child from bad companions or unscrupulous parents, or to give him access to a particular physician, teacher, or club leader.

Vocational Adjustment. In thirty-two instances a particular type of vocational adjustment was suggested, as illustrated by the following cases:

Hans O., a handsome boy of sixteen years, was found by psychological examination to have supernormal intelligence. He has worked for two years in a furniture factory at the very monotonous operation of feeding the planing machine. For eight hours a day he guided planks through a plane. In the evening he sought companionship and went out to "get some excitement," which of recent weeks had consisted of the daring sport of "borrowing" an automobile in which to go riding. The Clinic's advice was: "Hans should be employed in some business concern where he will have mental stimulation and an opportunity for advancement."

Lionel J., a finely developed colored boy, also ranks far above the average in general mental ability. He had completed the second year of high school, yet was not able to find any employment but shining shoes. He had worked at this trade since he was seven years old and was proud of his clientele and of the comparatively large amount of money he could make. He did his job well, but did not look ahead into the future. The advice was: "This boy needs some one to push him into a real job."

Mack I. comes from a fairly prosperous "middle class" home. His father makes a good income, his home is well kept and is located in a desirable residential neighborhood. Both parents are ambitious. They have saved money on which to send Mack through high school and college for they want him to be a "professional man." When Mack failed for the second time to get through the first year of high school, his father got him a job in the office of a friend and decided "to let him work until he comes to his senses and is willing to try in school." Mack ran away from home and was caught boarding a train with $50.00 that he had stolen from his father. The clinical examination revealed that Mack was not a deliberate loafer. He had tried hard to pass his examinations. His intelligence is little better than that of a moron. He can never graduate from high school—much less go to college. Vocational tests show that Mack has little chance of succeeding in his present job. Even clerical work is too difficult for him. The probation officer is advised to "start Mack in some simple trade and let him work up. But first make the family realize the boy's limitations. Care must be exercised to avoid their humiliation, and to elicit their coöperation."

Recommendations to Stop Work. In sixteen cases the advice was to stop work. More recommendations for quitting work are made for girls than for boys. Eleven girls are advised to stay at home and help their mothers or to be placed in foster homes where they will be shielded from bad companions and will be carefully supervised.

Hilda B. left her home in rural Nova Scotia to make her fortune in Boston. A distant cousin, Ellen, who had preceded her, helped her find work. Hilda was fired for inefficiency after three weeks. Ellen took care of her and again helped her find employment. When this procedure had been repeated three times, Ellen became disgusted and warned Hilda that she never wanted to see her if she lost her job again. Hilda, whose mentality is that of a nine year old child, was again fired. She did not dare go back to Ellen so accepted the hospitality of two strange men and lived with them for a week in a disreputable boarding house. The Clinic suggested: "Since Hilda has shown her inability to maintain herself in the industrial world, she must be persuaded to return to her home in Nova Scotia or to get a job as domestic servant. The probation officer should see that her employer is willing to give Hilda the supervision and guidance she needs."

In addition to the 100 children for whom work recommendations were made at the time of their Judge Baker Foundation examination, 60 children (54 boys and 6 girls), during the course of probation presented problems or needs relating to employment. What can the probation officer do to solve these problems? What resources are available? Is it possible for him to get jobs or to make adjustments for these 160 children?

PROBATION OFFICER'S METHODS

Treatment of employment problems, imminent and potential, begins with the clinical examination. Besides being tested, the child is questioned concerning his past and present work and his future plans. The very way in which these questions are stated as well as the reaction to their answers suggest standards to the child and may automatically change his attitude. Questioning may direct interest into fields never before thought of. The story of Sam M. illustrates a type of benefit incidentally resulting.

Sam M. was coached by his playmate whose Judge Baker Foundation examination preceded his by two days. He was told that everybody at the Clinic asks "What are you going to do when you finish school this year?" When Sam replied promptly, "Work," his friend warned him that such an answer would only bring upon his head a flood of other questions such as, "Where will you work?" "What kind of work would you like?" "What do you expect to do when you are a man?" These questions disturbed Sam. He turned them over in his mind many times during a sleepless night, without answering them satisfactorily. In the morning he hastened to the library and asked for "the book that tells you what to do when you are grown." The irascible librarian failed to sense a seriousness of purpose but concluded that his embarrassment was due to his presence there when he should be in school. She dismissed Sam and telephoned the school principal of the truant's whereabouts. The principal's anger prevented an explanation and closed the door to him as a source of information. Sam entered the Clinic in an anxious frame of mind. Without waiting for the question he said, "I don't know what I am going to do." The Director of the Clinic discussed possibilities with him and suggested ways in which Sam could get information on different jobs open to young men. During the six years that have elapsed Sam has come to the Clinic voluntarily three times and asked for vocational advice.

The probation officer capitalizes, where he can, this interest already stimulated and encourages the child to discuss his ambitions and future plans, causing him to bring under the focus of his attention vague ideas and dreams. This necessitates a decision or a recognition of indecision. But it also serves a more practical purpose. In the situation created by the sympathetic manner and sincere interest of the psychiatrist, judge, or probation officer, the child will express his secret aspirations—ambitions that he would never dare reveal to his companions for fear of being ridiculed or to his parents for fear of being scolded as impractical. Sometimes these ambitions are mere day dreams, impossible of attainment by the child; but more often the goals selected are within the realm of possibility, and can be attained if guidance is given.

The following case illustrates the rôle of the probation officer as guiding mentor.

Walter V. "never in his life got a decent deportment grade in school" according to his mother's report, "but recently his reports are so poor she has demanded that he stop school and go to work." The teacher reports, "Walter has a good head, but he won't apply himself. He fools all day with wire, knives, and string. Almost every day wheels, pieces of metal, and such things must be taken away from him before he will stop playing and concentrate. He seems actually to take pride in the fact that his writing is illegible. He is stubborn and uncoöperative. If reprimanded in school he truants the next day." The clinical examination showed him to have superior intelligence with special ability for dealing with concrete material. He completed the mechanical tests with exceptional speed and skill. After considerable questioning Walter confessed that his ambition was to become the world's greatest inventor. He was building a "radio machine" which would perform all kinds of superhuman feats. (Just what it would do was not definite in his mind.) He had rigged up an unusual mechanism in his basement and took smaller parts to school to work on in his spare time. On days when school was "just unbearable" or when he "had a new idea" he went off on long walks into the country to think out his plans. He had not told anyone of his "invention" because he had read about inventors' ideas being stolen. He had heard also that inventors never wrote

legibly and that they spent a great deal of time out of doors. When
he went for walks, he saw his own picture on the billboards as it
would be some day when he was famous. Here was a case for careful
guidance: an imaginative boy who recognized his own special ability
and who utilized it as a basis for a fantastic day dream. He used his
dream of future success as an excuse for retreating from reality. The
task of the probation officer for three years was to "bring him down
to earth." He helped Walter get a job in a garage where he worked
under the direct supervision of the foreman, a patient man and a
skilled workman who appreciated the boy's genius and who was
interested in developing his mechanical ability. The probation
officer secured special permission for Walter to take a mechanical
course not usually open to persons without high school training.
His work there was spasmodic; he tired of the prescribed assign-
ments and annoyed the teachers by "getting bright ideas and asking
foolish questions." But because of his spurts of good work and the
pleas of the officer he was allowed to remain. Walter is now in the
third year of a mechanical engineering course and has instituted
several improvements in method in the shop in which he works.

For every case where the employer coöperated, however,
five could be cited where they failed to coöperate. The employer's justification of this attitude is based on the idea that
refusing employment to persons with court records will act
as a deterrent to delinquency. This idea implies that the delinquent has sufficient perspicacity to foresee the results of his
actions for years to come. It implies, furthermore, that his
powers of social apperception are so acute that he will recognize the difference between behavior that conforms to "socially
approved standards" and behavior that violates them. Such
reasoning disregards the fact that what seems like deliberate
violation of law may be for the offender an attempt to win
approval by adhering to the codes of his own little group. But
even when there is a realization that truancy or stealing or
evading fares may get him into court, the young offender is not
likely to contemplate the effect such action would have on his
getting a job five years hence. The immediate desires for fun,
adventure, and "a thrill" are not to be compared as motiva-
tions of behavior with the remote possibilities of society's scorn.

Probation officers reported that it was very difficult to establish any kind of friendly relation between employers and probationers because of the common prejudice against "boys who are in the courts."

Friction between parents and children over the child's employment, unemployment, or wages also presents a serious problem to the probation officer. It is particularly difficult to bring about a satisfactory adjustment where despotic parents demand the wages of minor children; where rebellious children resent not being allowed to spend the money they have earned; where overgrown boys refuse to work, insisting that their parents should support them, or take the attitude, "the world owes me a living, why should I worry?"; where girls prefer to live away from home to escape parental supervision and boys want independence from their mothers.

The probation officer often finds it necessary to explain that the privilege of budgeting and spending one's own income involves one of the first lessons in values. The making of a budget necessitates the distinction between what is desired and what is necessary. One who suffers privation because of his own lack of self-control is likely to profit by the experience; the administration of his own wages teaches a child the limitations of its purchasing power and a better comprehension of the parental income. In this way his later voluntary assistance is more likely to be secured than if the parents demand his pay check "in order to teach him his responsibility to his family." The joy of earning is accentuated by the joy of spending, or at least the feeling that he has achieved something. He must not be deprived of the satisfactions resulting from planning the expenditure.

In solving the work problems the probation officer finds it necessary to use a large number of community resources. The list given below includes the resources most frequently used.

Resources for Juvenile Employment

1. Employment Bureau and Division of Vocational Guidance of the Continuation Schools.

2. Free employment bureaus operated by city and state.
3. Private employment bureaus.
4. Judge Cabot's farm at Holliston organized to give employment to boys needing training, outdoor life, or merely a place to live and work.
5. Social agencies, including family case work agencies, settlements, and clubs.
6. Caddy camps (to provide work, vacation, and training combined).
7. Members of the family, relatives, and friends.
8. Private files of persons needing help of a specified type.
9. Big Brother and Big Sister Associations (especially when a specified type of work is required).
10. State and national military training camps.
11. United States Army and Navy.
12. Advertised ranches.
13. Classified ads in newspapers.

Certainly, the probation officers exercised considerable ingenuity in helping boys to get work. One officer loaned money to a boy so that he could get a peddling license. Another made arrangements with a club leader whereby a girl could earn her club dues by addressing envelopes. A mother was persuaded to invest some money in a fruit stand to be operated by her crippled son, who had never been able to get a job.

Of the 100 Clinic recommendations 45 per cent were fulfilled, 30 per cent were attempted but not fulfilled, and 25 per cent were not attempted. Of the sixty problems appearing in court records during the course of probation 77 per cent were solved and 23 per cent attempted, but not solved. It is logical to suppose that many other efforts at vocational adjustment may have been made by the probation officers, but not recorded because of their failure to bring results. Since the resources consulted, the methods used, and the reasons for failure seem to be the same for all work problems, the two groups may be treated together.

The recommendation most easily fulfilled was "Get a job immediately." Where no specific kind of work was designated, the probation officers were quite successful. All of the girls and 63 per cent of the boys for whom immediate employment was suggested were placed at work. All children illegally employed were forced to stop work and all children who were advised to continue their education, to help their parents, or to go on vacations, complied to the extent of stopping work, but in only one-third of the cases was the plan advised fully carried out. Only one-third of the adjustments between parents and children, children and employers, and personality adjustments involving attitudes were achieved. Only 14 per cent of the specified jobs (apprenticeships, outdoor positions, and work in particular communities) were secured. The probation officers as a rule showed more persistence and more skill in getting jobs than in working out the subtle adjustments on the job. This fact indicates clearly that if probation treatment is to be successful either probation officers must be trained in the methods of social case work, or there must be closer contact between the officers and child guidance clinics.

The probation officer encountered failure almost every time he placed a "delinquent child" at a lower rate than the employer would have to pay for a non-delinquent on the assumption that the child would receive benefit from the supervision given. Instead of resulting in the use of toleration and patience, the knowledge of the child's previous stealing, sex misconduct, or stubbornness, seemed to cause suspicion and criticism of behavior entirely innocent. The employment of a child under this agreement was successful, as a rule, only where the employer was a special friend of the probation officer, or was a trained foster mother or a person with some previous experience in dealing with problem children. Again, some failures have been due to the fact that the officer's contacts with the employers were too infrequent, or that they did not explain fully enough the type of personal help needed by the delinquents.

During the course of the probation terms of the 500 children more than 200 different positions were secured. This tremendous achievement was possible only by the probation officers' extensive knowledge and skillful use of community resources.

OUTCOME IN RELATION TO PROBATION TREATMENT

Refusing to work seems to be considered by the court a danger signal, an abnormal reaction, a sign of an anti-social attitude, as shown by the number of cases where the judge says to the boy, "I will give you one week to get a job. If you do not work, you will be sent to training school." The probation officers seem to lose patience very quickly with a boy who deliberately gives up a job. The attitude of parents has been discussed.

There is a close association in the minds of most people between "refusing to earn an honest living" and crime. Every boy and every girl who would not work and who could not be persuaded to change an unfortunate attitude was considered a "failure" on probation. A total of twenty boys and seven girls were committed to state training schools because of their anti-social attitudes toward work, as expressed in earning money illegally (prostitution and homosexual practices) or refusing to work (giving the excuse, "It is the duty of my parents to support me," or "The world owes me a living"). In addition to these cases three boys and two girls who were not happy in their employment ran away and were not located by the Court.

On the other hand "having a job" is considered a sign of adjustment. Many records are closed with the statement, "Boy is now working regularly so his case was filed." A large percentage of the recidivists are young people who lost or deliberately gave up their jobs and drifted into further delinquency. More thorough investigation of the child's work situation might well have prevented his recidivism. The percentage of unemployment was almost four times as great among the recidivists as among the successful cases. If conferences with employers had been arranged, vocational misfits, "putting round pegs in square holes," might in some instances have been avoided. In other words the therapeutic value of having any job has been exaggerated to the detriment of both the job and the child. If a probationer desisted from violation of the law and worked regularly, his case was filed; if, on the other hand, he refused to work, the chances are two to one that he would be sent to a training school. This relation between "failure" and the fulfillment of Judge Baker Foundation recommendations is partially indicated by the following summary:

Recommendations attempted
     Recommendations fulfilled .... 6% failure (45 cases)
     Recommendations not fulfilled ...... 63% failure (30 cases)
Recommendations not attempted .... 47% failure (25 cases)

Likewise this study indicates a positive correlation between having a job and success on probation. The training value and emotional satisfaction resulting from well chosen work pave the way for future good citizenship. Certain benefits accrue from even the more casual jobs of running errands, selling papers, peddling lemons, delivering telegrams, groceries, milk, and ice, and caddying. In the first place, all of these jobs require physical activity in the open air. In the second place, they supply spending money that may be used for recreation or to supplement the family income. Expenditure of earned money develops discretion not incident to handling an allowance or pocket money obtained merely by the asking. In the third place, purposeful activity tends to prevent participation in mischievous and unlawful behavior. And, fourth, earning elicits parental approval and leads to happier family relationships.

The reasons for not attempting to carry out the recommendations fell into two categories. In some instances probation ended or plans were changed before the officer could act, as in the case of persons continuing their delinquency or responding so badly to other types of treatment that they had to be removed from their homes. In other cases the probation officer substituted another form of treatment for the one recommended, or concluded (as rarely happened) that no treatment was necessary, in which case he withdrew, leaving the child to manage his own affairs.

Children with deep-seated personality problems or with unpleasant family relationships should not have been released from probation merely because they and their parents claimed that work would solve the problem. The changing of attitudes is a slow, tedious process and one in which the probation officers showed remarkably little success. In many cases separation of parents and child was resorted to.

Since the records give little discussion of the purposes and processes, it is impossible to tell whether the failure of the probation officer was due to lack of skill, lack of persistence, or to other factors not discernible.

SUMMARY AND CONCLUSIONS

The preceding part of this chapter has shown that satisfying work plays an extremely important part in solving the problems of the delinquent. Although almost one-half of the children had already had either full-time or part-time employment, in only a few cases were their jobs suitable to their needs. The fact that so large a number of persons are without vocational advice and are forced to enter blind-alley jobs bearing little relation to their needs and desires should be of deep concern to the community. The case studies show that one-half of the delinquents during the course of probation needed vocational guidance or help in finding employment or in changing to work of a more desirable type. The maladjustment of one out of every ten delinquent children may be traced in part to unemployment, to employment under unwholesome conditions, or to anti-social attitudes toward work. Evidently more adequate machinery for vocational guidance and supervision and for occupational placement is needed.

The efforts of the probation officer were directed toward securing immediate employment for some probationers, vocational adjustment for others, and finally, cessation of work for others. In meeting these problems the probation officer has to consider the wishes of children and their parents and to adapt them to the opportunities afforded by industry. His success in making work adjustments demands a vast fund of knowledge of community resources and also professional skill in utilizing them. This study indicates more proficiency in the former than in the latter. Objective problems were solved more often and more successfully than subjective problems. The probation officer showed much greater skill in getting jobs than in making subtle adjustments involving change of attitude. Few of the conflicts arising in home situations over work were successfully dealt with.

A particularly crucial problem met by the probation officer was the unwillingness of employers to give jobs to delinquents. Both boys and girls when interviewed for follow-up reports said they were almost never hired if they answered in the affirmative the question, "Have you ever been in court on any charge?" Certainly employers (both in industry and in households) need to be educated to a better understanding of delinquent children and to a recognition of the assistance they could render society by taking a personal interest in them and by giving them encouragement and criticism when needed. A society that refuses to employ a person because he has a court record is inviting crime, because it makes it necessary for the person to seek a living by illegal means.

Despite these difficulties the probation officer was able to get 200 jobs for boys and girls during their probation. For those whose work recommendations were carried out only 6 per cent were failures as contrasted with 63 per cent failures among those for whom recommendations were attempted but not carried out. The far-reaching effect of this fact in relation to unemployment problems is self-evident. The large number of temporary successes in the first group presents another phase of the problem. "Success" in the sense of release from probation is related to "getting a job." But "success" in terms of continued good behavior is related to the individual's satisfaction in his job.

CHAPTER VIII

PROBATION AND EDUCATION

After the home, the school is the institution to which society looks for the training of its youth. It is pertinent, therefore, to ask, "Are the majority of delinquents still in school?" "Is delinquency the result of school maladjustment or school failure?" "Does probation lead to better educational adjustment? And if so, does school adjustment result in better conduct?"

When this group of delinquents came to the court, three-fourths of the boys and two-thirds of the girls were attending school. This fact in itself is significant. It means that these children are still under the supervision of the community. It means furthermore that school reports can be used along with reports of parents to gauge the child's progress. An inconsiderable number of children had stopped school to go to work, but were still attending continuation school. The re-

TABLE XVI

School status of 500 juvenile delinquents

	Boys		Girls		Total	
	Num-ber	Per cent	Num-ber	Per cent	Num-ber	Per cent
In School	299	75	63	63	362	72
In Continuation School....	15	4	2	2	17	4
Not in School............	86	21	35	35	121	24
Total..................	400	100	100	100	500	100

mainder of the children were adrift as far as the community is concerned. One eight year old boy had never been enrolled in school, but had managed to escape the truant officer by running away from home. Table XVI shows the percentage of boys and girls in and out of school.

The majority of the school children were enrolled in the regular elementary grades. Although about one-fifth of all children were classified by the Clinic as defective mentally, only sixteen boys and one girl were in special classes for subnormal children. Only 5 per cent of the boys and 12 per cent of the girls were enrolled in high school.

EDUCATIONAL PROBLEMS OF 500 JUVENILE DELINQUENTS

It is shocking that in a city with the supposedly excellent school system of Boston where many provisions are made for the individual treatment of the pupils, that the probation officer should be compelled to give his attention to educational problems. Yet two out of every five delinquent children showed signs of school maladjustment—unsuitable curriculum and improper placing as well as friction because of the lack of understanding. In addition to the thirteen boys and two girls who were considered by the Clinic institutional cases (see Chapter III, page 43), recommendations regarding school life were made for 114 boys and 34 girls. During the course of probation, the officers found it necessary to attempt school adjustments for 52 additional boys and 2 additional girls, making a total of 217 children whose educational problems were not being adequately met by the public school system.

The Clinic's suggestions may certainly be called progressive; indeed one may say daring. Educational institutions, nourished on traditional "principles" and bound by legal statute to circumscribed procedure, are requested to adjust themselves to the needs of individual children. These recommendations certainly follow along the lines of the most progressive experiments in education. They fall into four distinct groups as shown by Table XVII. The Clinic advised withdrawal from school for a small number of boys and girls, even

TABLE XVII

Judge Baker Foundation recommendations regarding school

Type of Recommendation	Number of cases		
	Boys	Girls	Total
Withdrawal from school to go to work..............	6	3	9
Change to a different type of school..................	43	14	57
Special class or special school for the retarded or mentally handicapped..................	15	4	19
Trade school or prevocational school..........	23	9	32
Rural or private school (in a different location)	5	1	6
Adjustment in the present school situation............	38	13	51
Adjustments involving change of curriculum, material or methods of instruction, training to meet a specific need as tutoring in subjects in which the child is deficient, etc...........	19	5	24
Adjustments involving personal relationships or a change of attitude......................	19	8	27
Supplementary education..........................	27	4	31
Continuation or return to elementary school for education beyond the legal requirement....	7	0	7
Higher education	20	4	24
Total.................................	114	34	148

though this was contrary to state school laws and special arrangements had to be made.

George H., a slouchy, overgrown colored boy of fifteen, was born in Birmingham. His father, who claimed to have murdered "two high yellow skunks who wanted his wife," was himself killed in a brawl when George was seven years old. Mrs. H., who was "smart and pretty as a picture," was remarried twice, but did not live for long with either husband. When George was thirteen, she came to Boston, accompanied by a "mighty fine gentleman." But this "gentleman" found George a nuisance and discouraged his staying around the house. George met "Slim the Gambler" and was admitted to membership in his gang. The mother does not appear to have been greatly concerned over George's gambling, drinking, or loafing, except when the truant officer approached her. When she was forced to pay fines for his non-attendance, Mrs. H. filed a stubborn complaint. When asked why he did not attend school, George replied, "That ain't no place for me." Since he was not mentally deficient, he could not be isolated but must attend the regular divisions, yet by achievement tests he was scarcely qualified for the third grade. Imagine this leering, dirty, profane colored boy in the third grade where he aroused the fear, curiosity, or disgust of the children about half his size. When he was examined at the Clinic, the directors warned the Court that "Society has not only a moral and criminal, but a eugenic problem on its hands. He should be removed immediately from a school situation in which the harm that he may do far outweighs any good to be derived by him. He should be required to apply himself to hard physical labor or must be permanently taken care of."

About one-tenth of the children were advised to change to a different type of school because they were not succeeding in the regular public school system, which seemed to offer no chance of progress. Of these, fifteen boys and four girls who were found to be defective and retarded in school were urged to go to special classes for the mentally handicapped.

Galileo B., age thirteen, had been in the fourth grade for three years and according to the teacher "knew less than when he first came." "Instead of trying to apply himself and catch up with the grade he spends his time shuffling his feet and making noise with his big, heavy shoes, or in printing his name on every page of his books."

Another group was urged to change from the regular curriculum to trade school or prevocational school. They were all dissatisfied in school and making little progress, but the basic reason for change was the existence of special abilities indicating their aptitude in working with concrete materials. The Clinic felt that the change might give them an impetus besides supplying them with useful knowledge. "Bean Pole" S. a tall, lanky colored boy, was urged to return to the South to one of the industrial schools for the colored. The Clinic suggested that two boys and one girl who were involved with bad companions in delinquency be sent away from home to private schools in order that they might form more desirable friendships. It was suggested that the probation officer secure rural boarding homes for two boys, that they might attend country schools. In small rural schools the group would be more heterogeneous and retardation would be less evident; and besides, children suffering from inferiority feelings would have more opportunity for ego satisfaction where standards were not so high as in the city.

In all of these cases the one goal to be attained is the substitution of satisfying and constructive experiences for socially undesirable ones. For example, the child who has taken refuge in day dreaming to escape from uninteresting textbook material must be given something to do that challenges him and is capable of holding his interest. Free time leads to poor mental habits as well as to undesirable actions. Too much pressure (too little time to accomplish the tasks assigned) leads to rebellion or to inferiority feelings. Hence proper school adaptation demands the placement of the child at the level and speed at which he can best work.

Other recommendations demand, not a change of school, but an adjustment in the same school. For a score or more children the treatment needed was tutoring in one or two subjects in order to be promoted, individual speech training for a little girl who lisped, and lip reading for children hard of hearing. Perhaps the most difficult task placed upon the probation officer was that of changing the attitudes of teachers and students in order to achieve the best results for nineteen boys and eight girls. It was necessary to secure the coöperation of teachers whose patience was exhausted with continued misbehavior and the lack of any response to their efforts. Two boys who had run away from home in June and therefore had not taken final examinations, were being required to repeat school work that they knew thoroughly. The Clinic, realizing both the waste of time and the danger to the morale of the boys, urged that the school authorities make exceptions to their regulations and allow these youngsters to be promoted on trial.

The suggestions for "supplementary education" include not merely the courses of instruction usually referred to as "higher education" but any education higher than the legal requirement. It really means "additional" schooling as it applies to boys and girls who had left or were contemplating leaving school when they reached the age or grade limit required by statute. It is noteworthy that even in this group of eighty-five boys and thirty-five girls under eighteen years of age who had discontinued school, only sixteen boys and two girls were advised to return, and the majority of them were recommended to take trade training looking toward better vocational adjustment.

Several of the recommendations described above are obviously designed to solve the problems of defectives, hence the question arises: "Are educational maladjustments peculiar to feeble-minded children or do children of normal mentality also have difficulties?" While the number of educational recommendations for defective children is proportionately larger than for normal children, it is no greater than for children of superior intelligence.

The following list shows the proportion of each intelligence group having educational recommendations:

JUDGE BAKER FOUNDATION CLASSIFICATION OF INTELLIGENCE
OF BOYS WITH EDUCATIONAL RECOMMENDATIONS*

GENERAL INTELLIGENCE	NUMBER OF BOYS WITH EDUCATIONAL RECOMMENDATIONS	PERCENTAGE OF TOTAL OF DESIGNATED CLASS
Superior	13	46
Good	32	27
Fair	22	23
Poor	26	33
Defective	34	47
Total	127	

* This list includes the 114 boys for whom specific educational recommendations were made and the 13 boys recommended for institutional care.

There are twice as many recommendations for the supernormal as for those of fair intelligence, and twice as many for the defective as for the fair. These figures confirm the impression often voiced in educational literature that schools have been organized to meet the needs of the normal child and have not made sufficient provision for the large number of children who fall above and below the "average." [1]

DOES PROBATION LEAD TO SCHOOL ADJUSTMENT?

In only one-third of the cases was the probation officer able to fulfill the educational recommendations, but with the minor educational problems that arose during the course of probation he was more successful. Of the 114 original recommendations 35 per cent were fulfilled, 21 per cent attempted, and 44 per cent not attempted, while of the later problems 77 per cent were fulfilled. It is easier to persuade children and parents that it is advisable to leave school than *vice versa*.

Parents show a strange inconsistency in their attitude toward school and work. They are opposed to their children's spending time in applied courses such as cooking, sewing, and manual training, partly, no doubt, because they consider the products useless. The recipes given by the Home Economics teacher call for ingredients that are not kept on hand; the bookracks and umbrella stands made by the boys are superfluous in homes that lack chairs and tables. But the chief reason why parents want their children to study grammar and algebra rather than cooking and carpentry is because they dream of seeing them in white collar jobs rather than doing manual labor. They have blind and unreasoning faith in the power of education to free them from arduous toil.

Two-thirds of the children who were counseled to stop school did so, but only one-third of the children who were advised to stop work and continue their education followed the suggestion. On the other hand, more than half of the children who were still in school remained for additional schooling as counseled, rather than dropping out as they had planned. The probation officer was especially successful in keeping in

[1] Sayles, Mary B., *The Problem Child in School;* Zachry, Caroline B., *Personality Adjustments of School Children.*

school children with high intelligence quotients. He needed
in most cases only to assure the parents that their child had
exceptional ability in order to win their coöperation. Teachers

TABLE XVIII

The efforts of probation officers to satisfy educational needs of 202 children

| Type of Recommendation | Recommendations | | | Total |
	Fulfilled	Attempted but not fulfilled	Not attempted	
Stop school	6	3	0	9
Change school	25	13	33	71
Adjustment	37	11	23	71
Supplementary.............	24	19	8	51
Total	92	46	64	202

and principals were eager to make concessions for "superior"
children.

The probation officer met with great difficulties in persuading parents to place their children in special classes or in
institutions for the feeble-minded. Parents object to any segre-
gation that attaches stigma to the child or to themselves.

Fiore W. was a pleasant-looking, curly-headed boy of thirteen.
He had repeatedly failed in school in spite of the severe beatings
that his father inflicted upon him after every examination period.
Fiore concluded that since he couldn't pass anyway and was sure
to get another beating, he might as well have as much fun as possible in the meantime. For two months he had truanted whenever
he could secure, by fair means or foul, the price of admission to a
movie. It was only after six weeks of intensive work on the part of
the probation officer that the parents allowed him to be transferred
to a special class and were convinced that encouragement would
improve Fiore's grades more than beatings.

Treatment that involved waiving of school regulations
seemed especially difficult for the probation officer. In the

few cases recorded where the probation officer presented the problem fully to the school authorities, exceptions were made —that is, dull delinquents were allowed to drop school and go to work without completing the legal requirements; children living in one school district were allowed to transfer to a school in another district to be separated from bad companions; boys and girls of exceptional ability were allowed to skip grades, or to be promoted without the required grades or examinations. On the whole, however, probation officers hesitate to approach the schools with these requests. It is impossible to say whether this reluctance was caused by discouragement from the teachers, whether the school system is too inflexible, whether special opportunities are too limited, or whether the school feels too little responsibility towards the delinquent.

Table XIX summarizes the results of the probation officers' efforts to improve the school status of 202 boys and girls.

TABLE XIX

Probation treatment in relation to outcome for 202 boys and girls presenting educational problems

	Permanent Success	Temporary Success	Failure	Unknown	Total
Treatment attempted: Fulfilled..............	52	28	11	1	92
Not fulfilled	16	20	10		46
Treatment not attempted	23	18	22	1	64
Total	91	66	43	2	202

DOES SCHOOL ADJUSTMENT RESULT IN BETTER CONDUCT?

Educational adjustment bears a unique and highly significant relationship to the incidence of delinquency. Table XIX shows that favorable outcome follows the fulfillment of education recommendations. Of the ninety-two boys and girls for whom probation brought about desired changes in the school situation fifty-two have given no further trouble to date and only eleven were failures. The results of poor school adjustment are not always evident immediately, but are none the less important. Where school recommendations were not carried out, the proportion of temporary success is higher than for any other group. These findings suggest that the needs which were discovered by the Clinic may not have seemed of tremendous importance to the probation officer, to parents or to school authorities, yet in the long run they contributed to anti-social behavior. The percentage of failure is twice as high where recommendations could not be carried out as where they were, and three times as high among those cases where treatment was not attempted.

Due to the efforts of the probation officer, thirty-eight boys stopped truanting and perhaps many others were prevented from truanting; some because interest in school was stimulated by a change of program or by the personal attention of the teacher, and some because of the fear of the consequences. Even in the latter case, school attendance resulted in a decrease of "excessive" movie attendance, loafing, petty street stealing, and begging. Regular school attendance brought good results indirectly in the separation from bad companions and in the development of extracurricular interests such as reading and athletics. But perhaps most significant of all is the fact that a few probationers, through their contacts with the Clinic, the judge, probation officers, and the principals and teachers of the schools, have been made to appreciate their own capabilities, have had revealed to them opportunities for their development, and have been stimulated by the desire to plan for themselves and to strive to attain useful positions in society.

SUMMARY AND CONCLUSIONS

Three-fourths of the boys and two-thirds of the girls studied were still attending school. Of these more than one-half were unhappy in school whether because of curricula ill adapted to their needs or because of attitudes incompatible with school adjustment. The operation of these same factors undoubtedly led to many others' dropping out of school and thus indirectly may have contributed to their delinquency.

Guided by the Clinic's recommendations, the probation officer effects the four following types of change: (1) Withdrawal of some children from school to go to work; this was recommended for a small number of boys and girls who were making no progress in school and whose wages were needed to supplement the family income. (2) Change to different type of school—to special schools for the feeble-minded, trade or prevocational schools for boys showing mechanical or other special ability, or classical high schools for youths who wish to go to college. (3) Adjustment to the present school situation by arranging for extra examinations, promotions or tutoring; or by solving personal difficulties arising between pupils and teachers. (4) Supplementary education. Less than one-half of the total educational problems were solved.

In some cases these changes necessitated radical deviations from the prescribed routine of the schools concerned, and success is closely correlated with the degree of coöperation given by the school principals and teachers. Parental coöperation likewise plays an important part in obtaining for a child proper school placement. It is much easier to persuade children and their parents that it is wise to stop school to go to work than to induce them to stop work to continue their schooling. Parents are particularly sensitive to the stigma attached to special schools for the retarded and in a lesser degree to trade schools. This attitude made it difficult to secure for many retarded and defective children the type of training which would be most advantageous to them. The probation officer finds more ready coöperation of both parents and teachers in meeting the needs of the boy and girl with supernormal ability.

Of the ninety-two probationers whose school problems were solved 57 per cent were successes while only 35 per cent were successes when their educational needs were not met. Where educational recommendations were not carried out and yet the probation was ended, one-half of the boys and girls were recidivists.

It seems likely that much floundering and disillusionment might be prevented if their were a more definite connection between training for useful labor in the public school system and opportunity to extend this training into apprenticeships upon leaving school. However, a change of public attitude toward the value of creative toil is crucial.

CHAPTER IX

OUTCOME AND CONCLUSIONS

RESULTS OF PROBATION

Probation in its best sense has not even been tried. Yet the probation officers, despite the many limitations of their work, as described in the foregoing chapters, achieved a remarkably high degree of success in dealing with these 500 delinquents.

Three major groups emerge when all the records are analyzed. One that is permanently cured of misbehavior, one that is temporarily cured, and one that is not affected at all. The following list shows the percentage of boys and girls in each group.

	PERCENTAGE	
	Boys	Girls
Permanent success	43	76
Temporary success	34	12
Failure	21	12
Undetermined	2	0
Total	100	100

For almost one-half of the boys (43 per cent) and for three-fourths of the girls (76 per cent) probation treatment yields the desired results, that is, it not only eliminates illegal and anti-social activities, but it prevents their recurrence. The word "permanent" as used here does not imply that the child cannot or will not misbehave again; it means only that from the date his probation ended to the time of the completion of this study (that is, for from five to seven years), he has desisted from misconduct. For a smaller group (34 per cent of the boys and 12 per cent of the girls) the probation experience results only in a temporary cessation of delinquency. That is to say, more than one hundred boys and girls dismissed

by the Court as being able to survive without its further supervision were returned to the Court as delinquents. In some cases,
new elements in the life situation of the child may have caused
later delinquency. But in the majority of cases recidivism is
due, not to different causations, but to the perpetuation of the
same detrimental conditions or influences that caused the first
delinquency. The frequency with which the same companion
accompanies the delinquent in his crimes, together with other
evidence, seems to attest this statement.

With the exception of five boys who were, at last report,
still under the supervision of the Court and of three boys
who died during their probation term, the remainder of the
children (21 per cent of the boys and 12 per cent of the girls)
continued their delinquency. The Court was forced to admit
its inability to cope with the situation. The children either
ran away and eluded the probation officers or they refused to
coöperate, in which case they were committed to state training
schools.

Not all children stop their misbehavior as soon as they are
taken to court. The elimination of anti-social attitudes and the
building up of a stable moral code require time and persistent
effort. A total of sixty-one boys and seven girls were returned
to court for crimes committed during their probation terms.
Of these, twenty-five boys were rated successes and the remainder, temporary successes. Their offenses were not always
the same, though a strong tendency prevailed for boys who
were first convicted of theft to reappear on the same charge and
for girls guilty of sex offenses to continue this type of misbehavior. The mischief and depredation of gangs seem likely
to continue unless the gang is broken up, and this depends
largely upon removing the leader and supplying substitutive
interests for the followers. Where nothing is done, gangs continue their pranks regardless of the "court experience."

An analysis of individual cases indicated that more than
half of the cases (61 per cent) reappeared in court either
within the first month of probation or after an interval of
irregular contacts with the probation officer. Where the pro-

bation officer was able to begin treatment immediately, the chances for reformation were far greater than where he was forced to delay. The coöperation of both child and parents depends upon prompt action, hence it is imperative that the court staff be sufficiently large to meet problems as they arise.

Violation of the law leading to rearrest is not the only criterion of maladjustment. A child who stops stealing but withdraws into a shell and indulges in a fantasy-life or becomes irritable, should cause as much concern to the probation officer as the child who continues his stealing because he needs or wants the stolen articles and knows no other way of getting them. The persons treating juvenile delinquency must not be misled by the disappearance of the symptoms of maladjustment but must be certain that the causes have been eliminated. The Court certainly viewed repeated delinquency with apprehension. Only 38 per cent of the boys rearrested as compared with 83 per cent of the boys who did not openly violate the law were released from probation in less than one year.[1] Recidivism certainly is related to outcome. Of the children who discontinued delinquency when placed on probation 40 per cent of the boys and 12 per cent of the girls were later returned to the Court. But of the persons filed as failures 95 per cent of the boys and 83 per cent of the girls continued in misbehavior more or less steadily to date.

Of the 220 boys who were recidivists during and after probation, the sentences were as follows:

Massachusetts Reformatory 19
State training schools (Lyman or Shirley)........ 51
Disciplinary school 2
House of correction 10
Probation 89
Fines or jail or both 49
                                          ——
Total 220

[1] The 400 boys were under the supervision of probation officers for a total of 3574 months or an average of 8.94 months. The 100 girls were under supervision for 1000 months or an average of 10 months each. The probation terms ranged in length from two weeks to three years. The length of probation term bears no relation to outcome.

Of the twenty-four girls who were recidivists, two are now in Massachusetts Reformatory for Women, twelve were sent to Lancaster, the Industrial Training Schools for Girls, and ten were sent to Bethesda, the House of the Good Shepherd, or other institutions for the care of delinquent girls.

OUTCOME AND PRE-PROBATION FACTORS

Society rightfully demands an answer to the crucial question: "Is success on probation due to differences in personality make-up and previous experience of the delinquents, or is it due to probation treatment?" In answer to this important question two types of data are presented: first, the relation between outcome and pre-probation factors; and second, the relation between outcome and the specific treatment given by the probation officer.

The pre-probation factors which seem of most value for identification and comparison with other groups may be summarized as follows:

This particular group is composed of 400 boys and 100 girls. The average age of the boys is thirteen years and of the girls, fourteen years. Nine-tenths of the delinquents were born in the United States, but only two-tenths of the parents were native born. They represent thirty different racial and national backgrounds. Many of the boys and girls live in "foreign" neighborhoods and only one-third of the parents speak English. Four-fifths of the homes feel the pressure of economic need, a third of them being at the poverty level. One-half of the delinquents are surrounded by "bad neighborhood conditions," that is, neighborhoods in which bootlegging, drinking, accosting, or gambling are openly practised or where low standards sanction profanity, vulgarity, and flagrant violation of the law. Two-fifths of the girls and a slightly smaller proportion of the boys come from broken homes; one-fifth of the mothers work away from home regularly and a slightly larger number work away from home occasionally.

Only one-fifth of the group is found to be physically sound

and in good condition; one-tenth suffered from major physical handicaps such as heart or glandular malfunctioning, tuberculosis, or digestive disorders. The majority of the boys and girls present minor defects or diseases such as carious teeth, enlarged tonsils, astigmatism, and mild cases of malnutrition.

Four-fifths of the children have normal mentality, but almost one-fifth are definitely feeble-minded. Almost two-fifths show "abnormal" personality characteristics or emotional reactions, but none are definitely psychotic. One-fourth of the boys and one-third of the girls have dropped out of school, and the majority of them have found places in industry. An equally large number have held part-time jobs, but few of the regular or occasional workers were engaged in work fitted to their needs. Many of the delinquents were definitely unhappy in their jobs.

Nine-tenths of the delinquents have companions who are also delinquent. More than three-fourths of all offenses are committed in the company of delinquent allies, or at the instigation of older persons. The lone offender engages in more serious crimes than the gang. Offenses are most often committed during leisure time or when unemployed. Less than one-sixth of the group have adequate recreations; two-fifths of the entire number report "street life" as their chief pastime; one-fifth give sex activity as their major or only pleasure. One-third are club members, about half of whom attend their club regularly.

Only a few of these factors have been proved to have a bearing on success and failure. Girls are more hopeful than boys, and children under thirteen more promising than boys and girls thirteen and over. No significant difference is found between delinquents from normal and from "broken" homes, but the young people with poor parental control show four times as high percentage of failure as those with normal parental control. Bad companions previous to probation do not influence unduly their outcome, but persons who have engaged in "vicious" recreations have only one-half as many "successes" as those with "good" recreation previous to probation. Physical condition bears no relation to outcome, but the mental and emotional state of the delinquent is very significant. Only one-fifth of the delinquents with abnormal personality traits were successes.

Outcome is not related to type of offense, but to length of time the offender has been consciously violating social standards. The boys and girls who are first offenders have twice as many chances of success as those who have been engaging in delinquency for a year or more. The lone offender is least hopeful from the point of view of probation. Only 42 per cent of the delinquents who committed their offenses alone were successes as compared with 70 per cent successes of the boys and girls engaging in crowd affairs. Race, nationality, religion, mentality, and work experience do not in themselves determine outcome. The most significant fact with regard to pre-probation factors is: *No one element or combination of elements discovered by this investigation can definitely preclude the possibility of success.* The Clinical prognosis proves to be by far the best basis of prediction. More than 60 per cent of all the Judge Baker Foundation's prognoses were accurate. Where the prognoses for boys were good, only 9 per cent were failures, and where the prognoses for girls were good, there were no failures.

OUTCOME AND PROBATION TREATMENT

The effects of probation treatment can be interpreted objectively only in terms of specific problems and the extent to which they were solved.

The social treatment conducted by the probation officer is concerned chiefly with five major phases of the child's life: (1) his home situation—the place and conditions under which he lives; (2) his physical and mental health; (3) the use of leisure time—his companions and recreational activities; (4) his education; and (5) his experience in earning a livelihood.

Where the home and neighborhood situation is inadequate or menacing, the three most effective types of treatment are:

(1) sending the child away from home; (2) persuading the family to move to a neighborhood where standards are higher and the dangers less imminent; and (3) case work on the family. Separation of the delinquent from his home is the most drastic act administered by the probation officer. This type of treatment was resorted to for seventy-six boys and girls, usually when they did not respond to other efforts of the probation officer, or when parents refused to coöperate. An equally large number were separated from their homes temporarily in order to carry out other types of treatment; namely, medical care, psychotherapy, or recreation such as that afforded by camps. The success of these cases depended upon the extent to which the specific aims were fulfilled.

Of the eleven delinquents for whom the Clinic prescribed institutional training ten failed to respond to probation treatment and had to be committed. On the other hand the probation officers, by following closely the guidance of the Clinic and by patient and careful supervision, succeeded admirably in their treatment of the fifteen mental defectives for whom institutions for the feeble-minded were recommended. That ten were successfully handled by probation indicates the value of preventive work among the feeble-minded showing delinquent tendencies.

The transplanting of the whole family to a new neighborhood is a valuable technique for removing the child from undesirable influences and for providing more wholesome environment. One-eighth of all the families were persuaded or forced to move to more desirable communities. In 60 per cent of these cases probation was successful. Where the families were urged to move and did not, the percentage of success was not half so great. Moving proved to be especially advantageous as a means of freeing small boys from the influences of bad companions. Both foster home placement and moving were used by the probation officer to impress upon parents the necessity to provide wholesome environment and thoughtful supervision of their children.

Many of the delinquent's problems are directly related to

elements within the home situation. In 122 cases the Clinic advised case work on the family. In fifty-eight of these homes the probation officer followed the suggestions. Here the difference in outcome is most significant. The entire group were filed as successes and only one boy has to date been guilty of delinquency. Where the probation officer could not solve the problems within the family group, the percentage of failures was four times that of success. The findings suggest an urgent need for more highly specialized training of probation officers or for more direct contact with case working agencies.

Through the efforts of the probation officers more than one-half of the group received medical attention. About one-tenth were treated for serious organic disorders or diseases, but the greater part needed glasses, dental work, fresh air, proper nourishment, or treatment for nose or throat difficulties. Probation officers often used medical treatment as a means of winning the coöperation of parents and as an introduction to the discussion of behavior problems. The correction of physical ailments is an important step in the prevention of personality defects and abnormalities, yet the fulfilling of physical recommendations shows little direct relation to success and failure on probation. The author questions, therefore, whether the time of the probation officer should be utilized in this way.

The 207 delinquents who upon examination showed mental content or emotional reactions deviating from the normal, presented a serious problem to the probation officer. Although these children were kept on probation on an average of twice as long as those with no abnormal personality reactions, the percentage of failure was twice as great. Only one-tenth of the persons classified as having "abnormal reactions" were successful on probation. Not only are the probation officers not skilled in understanding and treating these subjective factors, but community facilities are very limited. Cases of disturbing sex ideation and of delinquent ideation resulting from experience or from stories and movies of crime were more successfully dealt with than were cases of conflict over unpleasant family relationships, "inferiority complexes," and "emotional instability." In addition to psychotherapy and case work on the family, supplying adequate recreations, satisfying work, more admirable companions, or a more respectable habitat helped to restore normal emotional life.

While delinquents seldom blame companions for their own misbehavior even when they are caught together, yet they often admit that they cannot "go straight" as long as they associate with certain persons. Although parents frequently know nothing about their children's associates, they usually attribute any delinquency to the influence of "bad companions" whom they wish removed from the neighborhood. In 197 cases the probation officer attempted to eradicate the influence of bad companions or to prevent association. Two types of treatment were employed: in "prohibitive" treatment the officer says, "You must not be seen with John S. again"; in "constructive" treatment new companions or substitutive interests are provided. Where there is a necessity for immediate severing of friendly relations, geographic separation is the most effective method. The probation officer may remove the leader of the gang or may send the delinquents under consideration to a foster home, camp, private school, farm, or to relatives. Or, as stated above, moving may prove the solution, especially for children under thirteen. In all cases younger children were more easily divested of bad associates than older children. Where companionship problems were solved by the probation officer, 59 per cent were successes and only 4 per cent failures; and the offenses of those rated "temporary successes" did not occur until a considerable period of time after probation ended. *Where the companionship recommendations could not be carried out, the percentage of failure was ten times as great.* The offenders who had been tools or pupils of unscrupulous adults were all successful in outcome. The solution here involved substituting constructive influences for harmful ones. Throughout this study, instances appear indicating that the individuals who are most suggestible and who therefore respond most easily to "bad" influences are the ones who respond most quickly to "good" influences.

A large proportion of the delinquents needed help in solving their vocational problems. Sixty-five boys and girls were unemployed. Of the 108 who had stopped school and "gone to work" only seven could be classified as having "adequate vocational adjustment." Family conflict in a score or more homes centered around the question of the offender's right to work or not to work. To meet these diversified needs the probation officer attempts three types of treatment: (1) employment for those who need jobs immediately; (2) vocational adjustment to give opportunity for the greatest possible use of capabilities; and (3) cessation of work for probationers illegally employed and for boys and girls who might use their time more advantageously at home or by returning to school. The clinical examination is especially valuable in work adjustment; indeed, the judge sent some delinquents to the Clinic specifically that he might get advice regarding the type of work for which they were best fitted. In addition to learning his special abilities and disabilities, the boy or girl is benefited by having new vocational possibilities opened up for him and by having an opportunity to make articulate his secret ambitions.

Success in solving work problems depends largely upon the probation officers' knowledge of community resources and their skill in using them. The officers dealt with in this study showed exceptional ingenuity in the former. During the course of the probation, the officers secured more than 200 jobs for 500 children. In contrast to the present universal unemployment it seems remarkable that not once did an officer report that he could not find a job for a boy or girl who wanted work. On the other hand, the more subtle problems of placement were much less successfully met. Only one-seventh of the boys and girls needing a specified type of work were employed. In only one-third of the cases were adjustments involving attitudes effected. The probation officer was especially unsuccessful in solving the conflicts between parents and children that demand skilled case work to bring about an agreement of attitude. Employers were not inclined to coöperate; usually they refused employment to youths known to have court records.

This apparent close relation between employment and success on probation may be slightly exaggerated by the usual attitude of the Court. "Having a job" seems to have been interpreted as a favorable basis of prognosis, if one can judge from the frequency with which the following statement appears: "The boy is now working regularly. Case filed." On the other hand, refusing to work is regarded as a danger signal by parents, probation officers, and judges. *Every probationer who refused to work was classified as a failure. And the percentage of failure was ten times as great where work recommendations could not be carried out as where they were fulfilled.* The two most obvious needs in relation to satisfactory work adjustment of delinquents are: (1) enlightened public opinion regarding the joy of work commensurate with one's ability and the willingness of employers to give the delinquent a chance instead of driving him into anti-social behavior by excluding him from the privilege of earning an honest living; and (2) more skillful treatment by the probation officer in handling the subtler phases of vocational adjustment, and more attention given by him to the satisfaction that a given job can yield.

Since less than one-sixth of the delinquents had adequate recreation, the probation officers spent a great deal of time in trying to remedy this condition. Two different types of treatment appear. First, the probation officer tries to eliminate or modify: (1) those pastimes which are prohibited by law, such as loafing, bunking in parks and public places, improper sex activities, drinking and gambling; and (2) other activities that show a high correlation with delinquency, as, for example, excessive attendance at movies and burlesque shows, "street life," reading of obscene and sensational books and magazines, and "joy-riding" at night without the consent of parents. The second type of treatment consists in developing constructive interests including club activities, good reading, camp life, or sports such as swimming, skating, hiking, football, baseball, and hockey. Where a close contact is established between the probationer and a good club leader, the outcome is usually a happy one. Sending boys and girls for vacations in the mountains, to the seashore, to farms or to caddy camps brings very good results. In addition to providing the needed recreational outlets this treatment results in improved physical condition, separation from bad companions or from unwholesome home or neighborhood influences, and gives opportunity for the development of desirable social attitudes under the guidance of skilled camp directors or foster parents. The probation officer can do much to encourage parents to provide games in the home and to plan picnics, outings, and parties for the family group. His influence extends to community agencies and he can secure through budget appropriations or through private means the use of vacant lots for playgrounds and ball fields. Through these methods the recreation status of one-third of the 500 delinquents was improved while on probation. The proportion of success was twice as great where the recreation recommendations were carried out as where unsuccessful attempts were made. The accomplishment of the "constructive" type of treatment bears a closer relation to success than the carrying out of "prohibitions." The eradication of bad habits does not automatically result in the development of good ones. Better results in both kinds of treatment were obtained with the younger age group. In no case was recreational adjustment made for a person with abnormal personality traits. Many other facts point to the conclusion that recreation treatment can be used more effectively as a means of preventing delinquency than as a means of reforming the delinquent. Only one-fourth of the persons engaging in vicious recreations discontinued them to take up the pastimes suggested by the probation officer. The majority of this group were failures. On the other hand, the probation officers had remarkable success in developing good recreational habits for children who had no very definite program either good or bad. Over 80 per cent of them were successes.

Inability to meet recreation needs was due to: (1) lack of

facilities for non-commercial amusement and play; (2) unwillingness of settlements and clubs to grant membership to boys and girls with a court record; (3) lack of coöperation of parents and their failure to understand the importance of constructive leisure time activities; and (4) lack of technique on the part of the probation officer in dealing with anti-social attitudes and his failure (in some cases) to sense the needs of the individual.

That two-fifths of the 500 delinquents present educational problems should cause deep concern to society. Almost twice as many educational recommendations were made for supernormal and defective children as for those of normal mentality (46 per cent of the supernormal, 47 per cent of the defective, and only 25 per cent of those rated good and fair in intelligence). Proper school adjustment means placement at the level and speed at which the pupil can work best, be he genius or moron. The clinical report indicated what changes should be made in respect to school placement and choice of curriculum in accordance with the pupil's special abilities and disabilities. It also revealed misunderstanding between pupils and teachers that impeded progress, and unfortunate attitudes toward school held by boys and girls and their parents. To solve these problems the probation officer is often dependent upon the coöperation of parents and of school teachers and officials. Of the 202 delinquents who needed educational assistance 92 changed their status in the following ways: 6 were persuaded to drop from school to get work and help support their families; 25 changed to special schools for the feeble-minded, to trade schools, or to high schools where particular types of training could be secured; 37 were enabled to progress in their work by special tutoring, make-up examinations, or extra help from the teacher, or by absolving conflicts arising in the home or school situation; 24 either returned to school for additional education or were persuaded to remain in school when they had intended to leave.

School adjustment bears a significant relationship both to immediate and to subsequent success. School problems which did not seem crucial to the probation officer made their appearance shortly after probation ended as "probable causations" of further delinquency. In the matter of school attendance as with "having a job" and "joining a club," outward conformity should not be mistaken for inner satisfaction. It is the latter and not the former which determines success and failure. When educational needs were adequately met, the percentage of permanent success was 57 as compared with 35 when treatment was attempted but not accomplished, and 36 when treatment was not attempted. Both the chapter on education and also the one on work indicated that underprivileged children need better educational and vocational guidance and a system of follow-up that might prevent the hopeless floundering of many youths when they get out of school, by directing them into lines of work for which they are best prepared.

PRINCIPLES OF PROBATION TREATMENT

Out of the analysis of probation treatment given in the preceding pages, the following general principles may be derived: The first essential of probation treatment is an intensive study of the delinquent. No plan can be made until the judge and probation officer know the interrelationship of the factors influencing the habits and attitudes of the child. The diagnosis of the delinquents' problems is a task too great to be accomplished by one person, least of all by the judge or the probation officer whose numerous duties seldom, if ever, permit the opportunity to become expert in this field. Hence the plan followed by the Judge Baker Foundation and other child guidance clinics of having a group of specialists work together with the Court and the parents seems a very advantageous method of procedure.

This intensive study of the delinquent proved invaluable in discovering the motivating forces underlying his behavior, his special abilities and his disabilities. The recommendations of the Clinic form a working basis for the probation officer's treatment. Especially significant is the fact that the Clinic prognosis proved to be the most dependable index of outcome.

The second step in probation treatment is the establishment of a confidential personal relationship between the officer and the family. No plan however complete or however well adapted to the needs of the individual is of any value unless the coöperation of the child and of his parents is secured. Although the number of court records giving detailed information regarding process is small, they furnish ample evidence that success and failure of probation treatment are closely related to the nature of the contact between officer and child or what may be called the "level of treatment."

The third essential to successful probation treatment is prompt action. Court appearance precipitates a crisis in the child's life. It is fraught with psychological significance. While the child and his parents have their attention centered on behavior, the program for future action must be inaugurated. In most cases parents or other members of the family, teachers, and club leaders have attempted to correct the child. In many cases he has been threatened, but threats have not been executed. Ineffective efforts at control have led the child to believe that he can always "get by." Hence it is imperative that whatever demands are made by the court be carried out promptly. Many facts point to the important conclusion that the sooner careers of delinquency are checked the more hope there is of reform being permanent. A longer period of supervision is required for the treatment of recidivists than for first offenders. Likewise more drastic measures usually have to be employed.

The probation officer is continuously faced with the dilemma: "Shall I work with the most hopeful and let the hardened, the less hopeful delinquents go their way? Or shall I spend only a little time on the less difficult cases so long as they commit no serious offenses while I try to protect society by keeping close watch on the most difficult cases?" So far as the present investigation throws any light upon this problem the more economical course seems to be prevention rather than reformation.

The future success of probation depends upon constant and critical evaluation of the methods used and the results obtained. The tentative conclusions expressed in this book must be regarded only as hypotheses to be tested by additional experience. Skill in treating behavior and personality problems will increase as probation officers and specialists develop skill in diagnosing them. As more is learned of the strengths and weaknesses of human behavior—the "plus values" and "danger signals" of personality and conduct—more efficient methods of using this information must be devised by the probation officers. Effective probation treatment depends upon the mastery of a large body of information and a system of skills and techniques, which are as essential to the probation officer as specific information and skills are to the physician and social worker. *Hence it is of paramount importance that the probation officer be trained for his job.*

THE PREVENTION OF DELINQUENCY

If society sincerely wishes to lessen its toll on human life, to decrease its bill of from three to ten billion dollars annual cost of crime, to lower its insurance rates by decreasing the amount of robbery and embezzlement, to safeguard its women and children, to lessen the danger of kidnapping, it would do well to dig at the very roots of the problem, to discover and cure the criminal in the early stages of his development.

Perhaps what is needed most of all is a high sense of honor in all things, an unwillingness to tolerate deviations of conduct. This means a more careful scrutiny of our own morals, a demand of honest service from our public officials, and a revaluation of national and civic as well as personal ideals.

One of the most important steps in the prevention of delinquency is a change of public opinion in regard to the young offender, more sympathetic understanding of his problems, more appreciation of his natural needs and desires, and a conscious effort on the part of parents, teachers, recreation leaders, employers, and citizens in general to give adequate opportunity for the development of desirable social habits and attitudes.

Society could undoubtedly prevent delinquency in many

cases by the utilization and development of social institutions and practices already known and already used to a limited extent. Based on the experience of these 500 children, and the investigation that was made of the children during the period of probation, it would seem that a community should endeavor to provide measures of the following order:

1. Parental education that will prepare mothers and fathers for the responsibilities of parenthood.

2. Adequate family income to provide the physical necessities for normal growth.

3. Periodic medical examinations for all children and free treatment where needed for physical and mental disease and defect.

4. Recreation facilities so that children during their leisure hours need not be subjected to vicious influences.

5. A school curriculum sufficiently flexible to meet the needs of the individual child and clinics connected with the school system for the diagnosis and treatment of behavior and personality problems.

6. Vocational guidance for all children and a system of follow-up that integrates school life with work experience.

7. Enlarged court facilities, providing quick action, first in the investigation of anti-social trends, and second, in the treatment of offenders. Smaller case loads for probation officers, giving them opportunity to keep in very close touch with the children where it is deemed necessary.

8. More adequate training of probation officers and more direct contact between the court and child guidance clinics.

APPENDICES

APPENDIX A

Selected Bibliography

Adler, Alfred, *The Theory and Practise of Individual Psychology,* New York, Harcourt, Brace and Company, 1924.

Judge Baker Foundation, *Harvey Humphrey Baker: Upbuilder of the Juvenile Court,* Rumford Press, Concord, N. H., 1920, J.B.F. Pub. No. 1.

Barnes, Harry Elmer, *The Repression of Crime,* New York, George H. Doran, 1926.

Breckinridge, Sophonisba P. and Abbott, Edith, *The Delinquent Child and the Home,* New York, Charities Publication Committee, 1912.

Burgess, E. W., "Is Prediction Feasible in Social Work: An Inquiry Based on a Sociological Study of 3000 Parole Records," *Journal of American Statistical Association,* March, 1929.

Burt, Cyril, *The Young Delinquent,* New York, D. Appleton and Company, 1925.

Cooley, Edwin J., *Probation and Delinquency,* Catholic Charities of the Archdiocese of New York, 1927.

Flügel, J. C., *The Psychoanalytic Study of the Family,* London, Leonard and Virginia Wolf, 1926.

Glueck, Bernard, "The Significance of Mental Hygiene in Child Guidance," *The Annals of the American Academy,* Vol. 121, p. 57.

Glueck, Sheldon and Eleanor T., *500 Criminal Careers,* New York, Alfred A. Knopf, 1930.

"Predictability in the Administration of Criminal Justice," *Harvard Law Review,* Jan., 1929.

Hart, Hornell, "Predicting Parole Success," *Journal of American Institute of Criminal Law and Criminology,* Vol. XIV, No. 3, Nov., 1923, p. 405.

Healy, William, *The Individual Delinquent,* Boston, Little, Brown and Company, 1915.

Healy, William, Clark, Eric K., and Kasanin, Jacob, *A Study of Abnormal Personalities,* The American Foundation for Mental Hygiene, Inc., 1930. (A paper presented at the International Mental Hygiene Conference, Washington, D. C., 1930.)

Healy, Bronner, Baylor and Murphy, *Reconstructing Behavior in Youth,* New York, Alfred A. Knopf, 1929. J.B.F. Pub. No. 5.

Hollingworth, Leta S., *The Psychology of the Adolescent,* New York, D. Appleton and Company, 1928.

Johnson, Fred R., *Probation for Juveniles and Adults,* New York, Century Company, 1928.

Lou, Herbert H., *Juvenile Courts in the United States: Their Laws and Practice,* Chapel Hill, University of North Carolina Press, 1927.

National Probation Association Year Book, 1924 to date.

Reckless, Walter C. and Smith, Mapheus, *Juvenile Delinquency,* New York, McGraw-Hill Book Company, 1932.

Sayles, Mary B., *Three Problem Children,* Joint Committee on Methods of Preventing Delinquency, New York, 1924.

The Problem Child in School, Commonwealth Fund Division of Publications, New York, 1929.

Shaw, Clifford, "Correlation of Juvenile Delinquency with Community Organization and Disorganization," *Proceedings of American Sociological Society,* Vol. XXII, pp. 174-179.

Delinquency Areas, Chicago, University of Chicago Press, 1929.

Slawson, John, *The Delinquent Boy: A Socio-Psychological Study,* Boston, R. G. Badger, 1926.

Sullenger, T. E., *Determinants in Juvenile Delinquency,* Omaha, Municipal University of Omaha, 1930.

Taft, Jessie, "The Effect of an Unsatisfactory Mother-Daughter Relationship upon the Development of a Personality," *The Family,* 1926. Vol. 7, pp. 11-17.

Terman, Lewis M., *The Measurement of Intelligence,* Boston, Houghton Mifflin Company, 1916, p. 79.

The Child, the Court and the Clinic (a symposium), New Republic, Inc., New York, 1925.

Thomas, William I., *The Child in America,* New York, Alfred A. Knopf, 1928.

The Unadjusted Girl, Boston, Little, Brown and Company, 1923.

Thurston, Henry W., *Delinquency and Spare Time,* New York, Columbia University Press, 1918.

Tjaden, John Christian, *The Causes of Delinquency in Boys of Superior Intelligence,* Board of Control of State Institutions, Des Moines, Ia., 1923.

Van Waters, Miriam, *Parents on Probation,* New York, New Republic, Inc., 1927.

Youth in Conflict, New York, New Republic, Inc., 1925.

White House Conference, 1930, New York, The Century Company, 1931.

Zachry, Caroline B., *Personality Adjustments of School Children,* New York, Charles Scribners' Sons, 1929.

Zorbaugh, Harvey W., *Gold Coast and the Slum,* Chicago, University of Chicago Press, 1929.

APPENDIX B

SCHEDULES

MADE BY AUTHOR FOR USE IN
THIS STUDY

*(Back of schedule is used for
follow-up information)*

White for Boys

No.   Name

JBF. No.   Name   Address   District   P. O.

Birthplace   Date   Ref. by   Date case filed   Sub. prob.

JBF. Exam. date   Sub. exam.   Vis.   Last inf. type   Date

Social Agencies

Parents-status   Race-Nat.   Age   U. S.   Citz.   Educ.   Relig.   Occupation   Deling. Disease or Defect

f.

m.

other

Household   Sibs.

Home   Nbg.   Comp.

Dev. His.   Physical Status   Mentality + Mental Life   Personality   School

Illeg.   Wt.   Vis.   IQ.   wk   Gr.

Ante.   Ht.   Tons.   Class.   At.

Nat.   S.   Th.   Spec. Abil.   Cond.

Inf.   N.   Nose   Spec. Dis.   Abn. traits

Ill.   D.   Ears   Learning

P.   Ment. Content   Work

Age began

Type

Leisure   Record   At. toward deling.   Habits

Club

Delinquencies   Age 1st deling.

Type 1st deling.

Court Record—Previous   Present   While on Prob.   Subsequent

Causations

Type R | Recommendations | Contact | No V | Level | Remarks | Result

P.O. Prognosis | Class | Result
JBF. Prognosis

Sources: MPC. | J.Ct. | JD. | P.O. | Conf. Ex. | Soc. Ag. | Set. | Sch. | Inst. | Par.O. | Comp. | Home | Fam. | P.

Blue for Girls

No.   Name

JBF. No.   Name   Address   District

Birthplace   Date   Ref. by   Date   Date case filed   Sub. prob.   P. O.

JBF. Exam. date   Sub. exam.   Vis.   Last inf. type   Date

Social Agencies

Parents status   Race-Nat.   Age   U. S.   Citz.   Educ.   Relig.   Occupation   Delinq. Disease, or Defect   Disposition

f.

m.

other

Household

Home   Nbg.   Sibs.   Comp.

Dev. His.   Physical Status   Mentality + Mental Life   Personality

Illeg.   Wt.   Vis.   IQ.   wk   School

Ante.   Ht.   Tons.   Class.   Gr.

Nat.   S.   Th.   Spec. Abil.   At.

Inf   N.   Nose   Spec. Dis.   Rep.—   Cond.

Ill.   D.   Ears   Learning   Abn. traits

P.   Mens.   Ment. Content

Work

Age began

Type

At. toward delinq.

Leisure   Record   Habits

Club

Delinquencies: Age 1st delinq.

Type 1st delinq.

Court Record—Previous   Present   While on Prob.   Subsequent

Causations

Type R

Recommendations

Contact.

No V | Level

Saw G.

Remarks

Result

P.O. Prognosis

JBF. Prognosis

Class

Result

Sources. MPC.   J.Ct.   JD   P.O.   Conf. Ex.   Soc. Ag.   Set.   Sch.   Inst.   Par.O.   Comp.   Home   Fam   P.

APPENDIX C

OUTLINE OF FAMILY HISTORY, PHYSICAL EXAMINATION AND PERSONALITY RECORD

used by

JUDGE BAKER FOUNDATION

at time the study was begun

J.B.F. FACE SHEET

Referred by   Case No.   Date

Home   Alias   Cross Reference

		Age	Place of Birth	Race	Religion	Occupation
1	Fa.					
2	Mo.					
3						
4						
5						
6						

	Children	Date of Birth	Place of Birth	School	Religion	Occupation
7						
8						
9						
10						
11						
12						
13						
14						
15						
16						

NO.	Address	Date	No.	Address	Date

Relatives	Connection	Address	Date

Confidential Exchange

Agencies and workers on the case

OUTLINE OF FAMILY HISTORY

(As obtained at the Judge Baker Foundation)

INFORMANT

Personal Appearance	Physique. Dress. Slack or clean. Note particularly signs of nervousness.
Intelligence	Approximate amount of education. Degree of native intelligence. Inferior mentality, dull, slow or quick-minded; average, superior, keen.
Manner in which facts are given	Freely or only in response to questioning. State if informant is evasive, on defensive, voluble; gives one-sided or exaggerated account, etc.
Reliability of information	Thoroughly unreliable, partially unreliable. Incomplete because handicapped by language difficulty, poor memory, lack of time.

FAMILY

Nationality

Religion

Date and place of birth

Present address

PROBLEM

	Reason for exam. By whom brought or sent. Present court appearance.
Court record	Give date and cause of each arrest, also disposition. Institutional career, etc.
Running away and bunking	No. of times. Length of stay. If in neighborhood or some distance. Whether return was voluntary or by police. If hardships were endured, etc.

PROBLEM
(*Continued*)

Stealing	When started. Extent. If at home or in neighborhood, serious or petty. Alone or with companions. If persistent; if always objects of value.
Lying	Extent. If chiefly in self-defense. If persistent and continued amounting to definite habit. Fabricator. Give illustrations.
Truancy	Grade in which it started. Probable cause. Extent. Alone or with companions.
Behavior	Outside of home. Give illustrations and state if informant believes child was changed much, if normal mentally.
Informant's attitude and explanation of delinquency	If delinquency is due to companions, attitude, etc.

FATHER

Name

Age

Birthplace

Number years in United States

Citizenship

Health	General health. Note physical defects. Sickness—severity, etc. Describe any head injuries, severity and after effects. Inquire particularly into migraine, fainting spells, nervous prostration, venereal diseases, tubercular tendencies.
Education	Age of leaving school and grade. Any education since, such as night school, etc.
Intelligence and Character	Give informant's estimate of this and supplement it by your own impression based on his earning capacity, interests, attitudes toward children, interest in family welfare, etc.

FATHER
(Continued)

Occupation	Number of positions held. Length of time in each. Kinds of work. Average earnings. Attitude towards work, etc.

Habits — Use of drugs—particularly alcohol. Give exact details of extent. If a steady drinker; over-intoxicated. Moderately alcoholic, periodic type. Excessive. Delirium tremens, etc.

Standards — Of honesty. Morality. Degree of irregular living. Note particularly hypersexualism.

Court record — State if negative. If not, give dates, causes, sentences.

FATHER'S FAMILY

Paternal grandfather and grandmother
Paternal uncles
Paternal aunts

If living, where?
Occupation, character, etc.
State number in family.
Give physical, mental, and moral characteristics and occupations.

Inquire carefully regarding insanity. Give details of psychosis, age of onset, diagnosis, etc. Mental defect, alcoholism, epilepsy, migraine, fainting spells, convulsions, venereal diseases, paralytic shocks (inquire age of first shock). Court records, nomadism, criminalism, hypersexualism, nervousness, etc.

MOTHER — Give same information as for father with special emphasis on number of hours spent outside of home after marriage, nature of work, etc.

MOTHER'S FAMILY — Same facts as for father's family. Family attitudes and relationships.

SIBLINGS	Give names and ages in order, including all still-births and miscarriages. For all children give age, grade in school, physical condition, occupation, earnings, present whereabouts and character. Note particularly convulsions, fainting spells, nervousness, chorea, school retardation, delinquent traits, etc.

DEVELOPMENTAL	Note unusual age in the case of either parent, physical and mental condition of both parents directly prior to conception or during pregnancy.
Ante-natal	Note attempted abortion. State if miscarriage preceded pregnancy and if so, state length of time prior thereto. If mother worked outside of home give exact nature of work, particularly contact with poisons. Note consanguinity. Note illegitimacy and its effects on mother. Note illnesses, migraine, nervousness, fainting spells, worries, injuries or shocks of mother. Give full description.
Natal	Full term or premature. Long or difficult labor. Instrumental or normal delivery. Use of ether. Resuscitation. Note any injuries or deformities, particularly of head. Give weight and size.
Post-natal	Breast or bottle fed. Age of weaning.
Infancy	Nutritional difficulties. Note particularly excessive crying, nervousness, temper tantrums. Convulsions (state if negative. If not, give full description of them—age of starting, severity, duration, etc.).
Age of talking	Describe any peculiarities such as undue slowness in forming sentences, etc.
Age of walking	If slow, state if handicapped by unusual weight, etc.

Diseases	Age when contracted. Severity, complications. After-effects. Length of time in hospitals or under treatment. Operations. Note particularly epilepsy, minor attacks, chorea.
Enuresis	State if negative. If not, severity, causes. Particularly note all head injuries. Give length of time unconscious and after-effects.
Puberty	Age of menstruation. Regularity, peculiarities.
Fainting spells Headaches Otorrhea	State if negative. If not, describe fully.

HABITS

Sleeping	Number of hours. If quiet or restless sleeper. Note particularly somnambulism or night terrors at any age and describe fully.
Eating	Appetite normal or poor. Meals at regular hours. Diet good. Note especially fussiness about food, etc.
Drinking	Tea or coffee excess. Number of cups daily. Use of alcohol, in any form or degree.
Smoking	Age of commencing, degree.
Masturbation	When first noticed. Where and when practiced. Extent.
Nervous habits	Nail biting, tics, etc.

SCHOOL

Age of entering	Include amount of time lost through sickness or truancy and reason for leaving. Grade attained. Grades repeated, cause.
Advancement	Graduate. State particularly dislike for or difficulty in any one subject.
Behavior	Complaints from teachers in detail. State particularly if due to restlessness, mischief, inattention, or bad attitude. Truancy.

WORK

After school	Give nature of factories, also kind of work
In vacation	done.
Type of work	Amount of skill required, etc.
Steadiness of employment	Length of time in various positions, reasons for leaving or being discharged. State if efforts were made to get new position.
Earnings	Amount, how spent, if turned in to parents, etc.

INTERESTS

Indoors
Approximate amount of leisure time spent at home.
How occupied?
Degree of interest in reading.
Kind of books preferred.

Outdoors
Clubs.
Sports, gambling, pool rooms, bowling alleys.
Note interest in movies. Effects.
Vacations; how spent.

COMPANIONS
Names. Stability of relationships.
Ages (if older or younger than children in question).
If always same group or different individuals. Voluntarily sought.
Types of companions, particularly those with court records.
Note particularly any bad companions in neighborhood at time delinquent career started, their apparent effect on child.
Inquire carefully whether there were any older men or boys with whom sex experience or bad talk occurred.

PERSONALITY TRAITS—in detail.

As shown in home
Attitude toward parents and siblings. If affectionate or indifferent.
Generous or selfish, helpful or lazy. Aggressive or reserved.
Irritable, sly, untruthful, frank, confiding, fearful, suspicious, grudgeful, day-dreaming, etc., or their opposites.

School re- actions	If ambitious or anxious to leave school as soon as possible. Interested or indifferent.
Social reactions	Honest, coöperative, egotistic. Leader of companions or suggestible. Note degree of gregarious instincts or desire to be alone.
Vocation reactions	If able to hold jobs and in good will of employer. Interest in work.
Court reactions	If frightened by court proceedings or otherwise. Attitude towards institution in detail.
Change of personality	In what connection, in detail.

HOME CONDITIONS	State if always at home with parents. Number of changes. Years at present address.
Stability	If parents were ever separated. Either parent married before. If child was ever placed out—if so, length of time, and locality.
Economic status	Property owned. Rent. Debts. State if poverty exists. Help by agencies, etc.
Physical conditions	Number of rooms for family. State if crowded. Sanitation, light, air. Interests at home, etc. Piano, furniture, books, etc. Give your estimate in parenthesis of hygiene, diet, general standards of living, etc.
Family life	Amount of time spent together. Note harmony. Effect of quarreling, etc. How evenings are spent. Does family ever go to beaches, etc. Note if child is spoiled, indulged, harshly treated.
Parental attitude	Give in detail methods of discipline used by parents. Note whether parents are interested, have child's confidence. Boy's companions. If parents allow children to entertain their friends at home.

Language used at home	Foreign or English chiefly. Cultivated, educated, or vernacular. State if at times obscene or vulgar language is used by any member of household.
Religion	Interest in church activities, religious training given child.

DISPOSITION

State if informant wants child to remain at home on probation or feels he ought to be sent away. If so, where. State if relatives to whom he could go, if parents can afford to pay board, etc.

What family or neighborhood resources in case child remains at home, special help from relatives, church, Big Brother, Y. M. C. A., Boy Scouts, etc.

PHYSICAL EXAMINATION

Name   Age   Date

———————————————— GENERAL ————————————————

Symptoms   *Observation*

   Headache   Cleanliness

   Pain   Complexion

   Vertigo   Skin

   Epilep.   Posture

   Constip.   Deformity

   Nausea   Stigmata

   Habits   Physiognomy

   Speech

———————————————— DEVELOPMENT ————————————————

Height   Ft.   In.   Weight   lbs.   Nutrition   Gen. Develop.
Pub.   Bre.   Muscular
Genit.   Mens.

———————————————— HEAD ————————————————

Eyes
   Vision ^R_L Pupil form   Fields
   Conjunc.   " react.   Ptosis
   Movements   Diplopia   Nystag.
                                      Strabis.

Ears
   Hearing ^R_L Otorrhea   Mouth

Teeth
   Crowded   Hutch.   Carious

Skull
   Contour   Circum.   Length   Breadth

———————————————— NEURO-MUSC. ————————————————

Reflex—Arm   Tremor   Strength ^U_L
   K. J.   Sensation
   Abd.   Gait   Coord. ^U_L
   Achilles   Clonus

———————————————— RESP. ————————————————

Nose   Adenoids   Thorax
Throat   Tonsils   Lungs

———————————————— GLANDULAR ————————————————

Thyroid   Adenopathy   Endocrine

———————————————— OSSEOUS ————————————————

Spine   Legs   Feet   Thorax

———————————————— CIRCUL. ————————————————

Heart   Color   Extremities

By

Personality Record

(1) (2) (3) (4)   Case No. ....

(5) Age of First Recognition of Personality Trouble
- 0. Under three
- 1. Three to six
- 2. Six to nine
- 3. Nine to twelve
- 4. Twelve to fifteen
- 5. Unknown

(6) Sex
- 0. Male
- 1. Female

(7) Racial Stock
- 0. Anglo-Saxon
- 1. Jewish
- 2. Celtic
- 3. Teutonic
- 4. Scandinavian
- 5. Southern Italian
- 6. Slavic
- 7. Negro
- 8. Mixed
- 9. Others

(8) Economic Status of Parents
- 0. Destitute
- 1. Poverty
- 2. Normal
- 3. Comfortable
- 4. Luxury

(9) Heredity of Parents or Siblings
- 0. Manic-depressive
- 1. Dementia praecox
- 2. Undiagnosed psychoses
- 3. Epilepsy
- 4. F. m. or dull
- 5. Psych. personality
- 6. Const. inferiority
- 7. Neurotic traits
- 8. Conduct disorder
- 9. Peculiar personality
- X. Negative

(10a) Parental Influence
- 0. Alcoholism of father at conception
- 1. Ill-health of father at conception
- 2. Miscarriage prior to pregnancy
- 3. Consanguinity of parents

(10b) Pregnancy
- 4. Alcoholism of mother
- 5. Drug addict
- 6. Other illness of mother
- 7. Attempted abortion
- 8. Congenital syphilis
- 9. Normal

(11) Birth History
- 0. Normal
- 1. Difficult or instrumental
- 2. Abnormal presentation
- 3. Premature
- 4. Weight below 5 pounds
- 5. Twin

(12) Illness of Infancy
- 0. Early malnutrition
- 1. Convulsions
- 2. Severe gastro intestinal
- 3. Severe infectious disease
- 4. Disease of central nervous system
- 5. Severe head injury
- 6. Rickets
- 7. Negative

(13) Diseases of Childhood
- 0. Chorea
- 1. Encephalitis
- 2. Meningitis
- 3. Tuberculosis
- 4. Epilepsy
- 5. Syphilis (Wasserman)
- 6. Otorrhea
- 7. Head injury
- 8. Others (severe)
- 9. Negative

(14) Habits of Childhood
- 0. Alcohol
- 1. Tea and coffee (excess)
- 2. Smoking (excess)
- 3. Sleep anomalies
- 4. Eating anomalies
- 5. Masturbation
- 6. Enuresis
- 7. Negative

(15) Earlier Neurotic Traits
- 0. Tics
- 1. Mannerisms
- 2. Excessive nail biting
- 3. Peculiar habits
- 4. Headaches
- 5. Fainting spells
- 6. Temper tantrums
- 7. "Nervous" (excess. fussy)
- 8. Others
- 9. Negative

(16) Puberty
- 0. Puberty (12 or earlier)
- 1. Puberty delayed (16 or over)
- 2. Normal
- 3. Unknown

(17) Physical Condition
- 0. Cons. oversized for race and family
- 1. Cons. undersized for race and family
- 2. Overweight
- 3. Underweight
- 4. Severe defective vision
- 5. More than slight defective vision
- 6. Strabismus
- 7. Anom. of sex develop.
- 8. Negative

(18a) Diseases
- 0. Heart (more than slight)
- 1. Diseased tonsils or adenoids
- 2. Badly carious teeth
- 3. Otorrhea
- 4. Syphilis
- 5. Phimosis

(18b) Neurological
- 0. Hyperactive reflexes
- 1. Tremor
- 8. Nervous disease
- 9. Dizziness
- X. Headaches
- △ Negative

(19) Special Stigmata
0. Hernia
1. Ears
2. Cranium
3. Palate
4. Endocrine
5. Negative

(20) Intelligence
0. Feebleminded
1. Subnormal
2. Poor
3. Fair
4. Good
5. Supernormal
6. Scattering in test
7. Irregular in abilities
8. Mental control poor
9. Poor apperceptions

(21) Personality Characteristics
0. Annoying others
1. Apathetic
2. Belligerent
3. Boisterous
4. Bitter
5. Bluffer
6. Childish
7. Contrary
8. Contemptuous
9. Cowardly
X. Cruel
Δ. Defiant

(22) Personality Characteristics (Continued)
0. Depressed
1. Desire for novelty
2. Desire for attention
3. Destructive
4. Day-dreaming
5. Distractible
6. Domineering
7. Disobedient
8. Disagreeable
9. Easily discouraged
X. Ego centric
Δ. Emot. labil

(23) Personality Characteristics (Continued)
0. Extrovert
1. Excitable
2. Easily fatigued
3. Fabricating
4. Fearsome
5. Feeling of incomp.
6. Frank
7. Feeling of inferiority
8. Fault finding
9. Fond of excitement
X. Gregarious +
Δ. Grudgeful

(24) Personality Characteristics (Continued)
0. Grouchy
1. Happy-go-lucky
2. Hedonistic
3. Hyper-suggestible
4. Impertinent
5. Inconsiderate
6. Impish
7. Impulsive
8. Irritable
9. Inabil. to follow goal
X. Indif. to moral issue
Δ. Irrational spells

(25) Personality Characteristics (Continued)
0. Introvert
1. Jealous +
2. Lazy
3. Languid
4. Lacking in enthusiasm
5. Lacking planfulness
6. Lachrymose
7. Lacking initiative
8. Lacking insight
9. Listless
Δ. Lacking persistence
X. Lacking in affection

(26) Personality Characteristics (Continued)
0. Morbid
1. Much complaining
2. Mischievous
3. Meddlesome
4. Meek
5. Morose
6. Not helpful
7. Not ambitious
8. Non-social
9. Over-confident
X. Over-modest
Δ. Over-active

(27) Personality Characteristics (Continued)
0. Obsessional tendencies
1. Obstinate
2. Perplexed
3. Passive
4. Poser
5. Quarrelsome
6. Quick tempered
7. Restless
8. Reticent
9. Resent. authority
X. Resent. criticism
Δ. Reckless

(28) Personality Characteristics (Continued)
0. Rebellious
1. Sullen
2. Sober
3. Solitary +
4. Stubborn
5. Sheepish
6. Self-abasive
7. Silly
8. Submissive
9. Sensitive
X. Suspicious
Δ. Shy

(29) Personality Characteristics (Continued)
0. Seclusive
1. Selfish
2. Shiftless
3. Suicidal tendencies
4. Self-assertive
5. Strong likes and dislikes
6. Sex preoccupation
7. Shy
8. Tense
9. Taciturn
X. Timid
Δ. Tender-hearted

(30) Personality Characteristics (Continued)
0. Untruthful
1. Unreliable
2. Uncleanly
3. Violent
4. Vain
5. Vindictive
6. Weak inhibitions
7. Variable moods

(31) Family Make-up
0. Father absent from hsld.
1. Mother absent from hsld
2. Step-parents
3. Only child
4. Oldest child
5. Youngest child
6. Illegitimate child
7. Adopted child
8. Hated child
9. Spoiled child
X. Negative

(32) Family Life
0. Excessive quarreling
1. Disharmony
2. Divided attention
3. Child imit. parent. cond.
4. Aber. person in hsld.
5. Poor parental control
6. Parental repression
7. Erratic behavior in hsld
8. Negative

APPENDIX D

FORMS USED
by the
BOSTON JUVENILE COURT

INFORMATION BLANK

2000—4-'29.

BOSTON JUVENILE COURT

Name   Birth and Place   **Pro. Off.**

Address   Floor   No. Rooms   Rent

Court	Date	Complaint	Disp.	Date

Parents	Birth and Place	Religion	Occ. or sch.	Pay	Remarks

Children

Church   Pastor   Club

School   Grade   Teacher   Date   Attend.   Scholarship

Relatives:

Employers:

Agencies:

History:

BOSTON JUVENILE COURT

To......................................

....

You are hereby notified to report at the office of
Dr. William Healy, Room 1214, 40 Court Street,
at...................*o'clock, on*............................

....

Probation Officer.

SCHOOL REPORT

———————

Name of School...

Name of Pupil..

For week ending..

    Attendance ....

    Conduct ....

    Scholarship ....

    Effort ....

    Signature of Teacher...............................

ANY ADDITIONAL INFORMATION WILL BE WELCOME AND
MAY BE WRITTEN ON THE BACK OF THIS CARD.

INFORMATION BLANK

Name..Birth and Place
....

Address ....fl.........rm.........rent
....

Parents ....Birthpl..............Rel.............Job
....

Siblings ....Age............................Job
....
....
....
....

Court ....Date..........Offence..........Disp.
....
....

Employers or School..........Date.........gr...........teacher
....
....
....

Church ....Club
....
....

Agencies ....
....

Court Cont. dates......................Doctor's Requirement
....
....
....

Sch. Reports................................Dates when rep.

BOSTON JUVENILE COURT

To..

The Court has put you on probation to give you a chance to make good. You must do your best to succeed in school and at work, at home, in church or temple and among your friends.

If you are making good, the Court will end your probation. If you are not, the Court may send you away to be trained.

Your time on probation is until.............

The Court may make it shorter or longer.

HOW TO WIN ON PROBATION

1. Keep yourself clean in body, mind and habits and win health, strength and courage.
2. Keep good hours at meals in the day and at night and win regular ways of living.
3. Keep friendly and helpful with your father, mother, brothers and sisters and win their pride in you and a better home.
4. Keep active in games and clubs and win good sportsmanship.
5. Keep good company with friends and books and win an idea of what can be done in the world.
6. Keep good attendance at every session of school and win a high mark for effort.
7. Keep at work for regular hours every day and win a place for yourself.
8. Keep strictly your religious duties and win reverence and faith.
9. Keep the law and the rules of the city and win as a good citizen.

BRING THIS CARD WHEN YOU REPORT

Report at ....

Day and hour ....

Reported on the following dates

January			
February			
March			
April			
May			
June			
July			
August			
September			
October			
November			
December			

Report immediately to your probation officer any change in your school, your work, and the address where you live.

The name of your probation officer is —

APPENDIX E

SUPPLEMENTARY GRAPHS AND TABLES

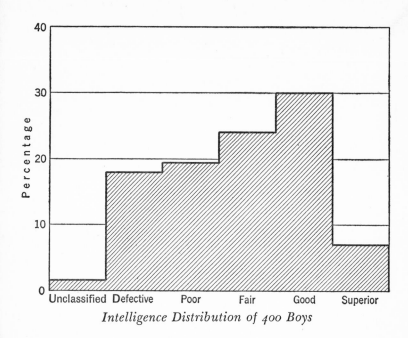

Intelligence Distribution of 400 Boys

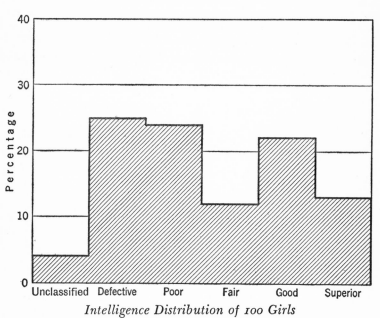

Intelligence Distribution of 100 Girls

TABLE XX

Outcome in relation to age

	Success		Temporary Success		Failure		Unknown		Total	
	Num-ber	Per cent	Num-ber	Per cent	Num-ber	Per cent	Num-ber	Per cent	Num-ber	Per cent
BOYS										
7 years to 10 years 6 months	34	49	22	32	11	16	2	3	69	100
10 years 6 months to 13 years 6 months.............,..	52	39	56	42	23	17	2	2	133	100
13 years 6 months to 17 years	86	43	57	29	51	26	4	2	198	100
Total	172	43	135	34	85	21	8	2	400	100
GIRLS										
7 years to 10 years 6 months	4	80			1	20			5	100
10 years 6 months to 13 years 6 months...............	18	75	3	12.5	3	12.5			24	100
13 years 6 months to 17 years	54	76	9	13	8	11			71	100
Total	76	76	12	12	12	12			100	100

TABLE XXI

Outcome in relation to place of birth

	Success		Temporary Success		Failure		Unknown		Total	
	Number	Per cent	Number	Per cent	Number	Per cent	Number	Per cent	Number	Per cent
Boys										
Boston...................	107	46	83	35	40	17	5	2	235	100
Massachusetts outside of Boston..................	36	40	27	30	26	28	2	2	91	100
United States outside of Massachusetts .....,....	14	42.5	10	30	9	27.5			33	100
Foreign country	14	38	14	38	8	21	1	3	37	100
Unknown	1	25	1	25	2	50			4	100
Total	172	43	135	34	85	21	8	2	400	100
Girls										
Boston...................	31	69	9	20	5	11			45	100
Massachusetts outside of Boston..................	27	85	2	6	3	9			32	100
United States outside of Massachusetts	11	92			1	8			12	100
Foreign country	7	70			3	30			10	100
Unknown			1	100					1	100
Total	76	76	12	12	12	12			100	100

TABLE XXII

Outcome in relation to race, nativity, language classification of parents

	Success		Temporary Success		Failure		Unknown		Total	
	Number	Per cent	Number	Per cent	Number	Per cent	Number	Per cent	Number	Per cent
Boys										
Both parents born in United States (white)............	25	47	11	21	14	26	3	6	53	100
One parent born in United States (white).............	8	36	5	23	8	36	1	5	22	100
Colored	9	41	6	27	7	32			22	100
Foreign—English speaking..	16	31	23	45	11	22	1	2	51	100
Foreign—South European..	79	47	66	38	25	14	2	1	172	100
Foreign—North European..	30	42	23	32	18	25	1	1	72	100
Unknown	5	62	1	13	2	25			8	100
Total	172	43	135	34	85	21	8	2	400	100
Girls										
Both parents born in United States (white)............	10	59	4	23.5	3	17.5			17	100
One parent born in United States (white).............	10	83	1	8.5	1	8.5			12	100
Colored	6	85	1	15					7	100
Foreign—English speaking..	14	74	1	5	4	21			19	100
Foreign—South European..	22	79	3	10.5	3	10.5			28	100
Foreign—North European..	14	82	2	12	1	6			17	100
Total	76	76	12	12	12	12			100	100

TABLE XXIII

Outcome in relation to intelligence

	Success		Temporary Success		Failure		Unknown		Total	
	Number	Per cent	Number	Per cent	Number	Per cent	Number	Per cent	Number	Per cent
Boys										
Superior	14	50	7	25	6	21	1	4	28	100
Good	54	45	36	30	26	22	4	3	120	100
Fair	37	38	39	41	19	20	1	1	96	100
Poor	34	44	23	30	20	25	1	1	78	100
Defective	29	40	28	39	14	20	1	1	72	100
Unclassified	4	67	2	33					6	100
Total	172	43	135	34	85	21	8	2	400	100
Girls										
Superior	13	100							13	100
Good	15	68	4	18	3	14			22	100
Fair	12	100							12	100
Poor	17	71	3	12	4	17			24	100
Defective	17	68	5	20	3	12			25	100
Unclassified	2	50			2	50			4	100
Total	76	76	12	12	12	12			100	100

TABLE XXIV

Outcome in relation to home status

	Success		Temporary Success		Failure		Unknown		Total	
	Number	Per cent	Number	Per cent	Number	Per cent	Number	Per cent	Number	Per cent
BOYS										
Normal home	112	44	97	38	44	17	3	1	256	100
Broken home...............	60	42	38	26	41	29	5	3	144	100
Total	172	43	135	34	85	21	8	2	400	100
GIRLS										
Normal home	46	76	7	12	7	12			60	100
Broken home..............	30	75	5	12.5	5	12.5			40	100
Total	76	76	12	12	12	12			100	100

TABLE XXV

Outcome in relation to parental control and supervision

	Success		Temporary Success		Failure		Unknown		Total	
	Number	Per cent	Number	Per cent	Number	Per cent	Number	Per cent	Number	Per cent
BOYS										
Normal control............	116	51.5	78	35	29	13	1	.5	224	100
Lack of control............	56	32	57	32	56	32	7	4	176	100
Total	172	43	135	34	85	21	8	2	400	100
GIRLS										
Normal control............	44	88	5	10	1	2			50	100
Lack of control............	32	64	7	14	11	22			50	100
Total	76	76	12	12	12	12			100	100

TABLE XXVI

Outcome in relation to offense

	Success		Temporary Success		Failure		Unknown		Total	
	Number	Per cent	Number	Per cent	Number	Per cent	Number	Per cent	Number	Per cent
BOYS										
Crimes against property....	135	44	105	34	63	20	6	2	309	100
Crimes against person......	13	46	12	43	3	11			28	100
Runaway and stubborn complaints...................	13	69	5	26	1	5			19	100
Statutory offenses..........	11	25	13	29.5	18	41	2	4.5	44	100
Total	172	43	135	34	85	21	8	2	400	100
GIRLS										
Crimes against property....	49	79	8	13	5	8			62	100
Crimes against person......	13	100							13	100
Runaway and stubborn complaints...................	11	55	2	10	7	35			20	100
Statutory offenses..........	3	60	2	40					5	100
Total	76	76	12	12	12	12			100	100

TABLE XXVII

Outcome in relation to duration of delinquency.

	Success		Temporary Success		Failure		Unknown		Total	
	Num-ber	Per cent	Num-ber	Per cent	Num-ber	Per cent	Num-ber	Per cent	Num-ber	Per cent
BOYS										
None previously	52	64	24	29	6	7			82	100
Less than 1 year...........	43	49	23	26	19	22	3	3	88	100
1 year to 5 years...........	61	33.5	73	40	43	23.5	5	3	182	100
Over 5 years..............	16	33.4	15	31.3	17	35.3			48	100
Total	172	43	135	34	85	21	8	2	400	100
GIRLS										
None previously	25	81	5	16	1	3			31	100
Less than 1 year...........	30	86	4	11	1	3			35	100
1 year to 5 years...........	17	63	3	11	7	26			27	100
Over 5 years..............	4	57			3	43			7	100
Total	76	76	12	12	12	12			100	100

Appendix E

TABLE XXVIII

Causative factors in juvenile delinquency (400 boys)

	Success		Temporary Success		Failure		Unknown		Total	
	Num-ber	Per cent	Num-ber	Per cent	Num-ber	Per cent	Num-ber	Per cent	Num-ber	Per cent
ENVIRONMENTAL										
Recreation................	51	38	48	36	30	23	4	3	133	·100
Bad companions	84	41	72	35	44	21	7	3	207	100
"Companionship affair"....	58	55	35	33	12	12			105	100
Lack of parental control....	58	33	55	31	56	32	7	4	176	100
Poverty	4	28	5	36	5	36			14	100
Poor neighborhood	19	38	21	42	8	16	2	4	50	100
Opportunity	14	50	11	39	2	7	1	4	28	100
Victim...................	2	50	2	50					4	100
Poor work adjustment.....	3	25	4	33	5	42			12	100
Poor school adjustment	3	75			1	25			4	100
Total Environmental ..	296	40	253	35	163	22	21	3	733	100
PERSONAL										
Mentality										
Supernormal............	2	100							2	100
Defective...............	20	41	15	31	12	24	2	4	49	100
Abnormal personality....	4	67	2	33					6	100
Personality traits..........	30	32	29	30	34	36	2	2	95	·100
Ideation and imagery......	64	38	50	29	51	30	5	3	170	100
Habits and experience......	37	40	26	28	27	29	3	3	93	100
Circumstances	4	66	1	17	1	17			6	·100
Physical make-up..........	12	43	4	14	12	43			28	100
Total Personal	173	39·	127	28	137	30	12	3	449	100
Grand Total.............	469	40	380	32	300	25	33	3	1182	100

TABLE XXIX

Causative factors in juvenile delinquency (100 girls)

	Success		Temporary Success		Failure		Total	
	Number	Per cent	Number	Per cent	Number	Per cent	Number	Per cent
ENVIRONMENTAL								
Recreation...............	10	56	2	11	6	33	18	100
Bad companions	37	73	6	12	8	15	51	100
Companionship affair	10	84	1	8	1	8	12	100
Lack of parental control....	32	64	7	14	11	22	50	100
Poverty	7	88	1	12			8	100
Poor neighborhood........	6	86	1	14			7	100
Opportunity	7	78	2	22			9	100
Victim...................	1	100					1	100
Total Environmental ..	110	70	20	13	26	17	156	100
PERSONAL								
Mentality								
Supernormal............	4	100					4	100
Defective...............	12	60	3	15	5	25	20	100
Abnormal personality	2	67			1	33	3	100
Personality traits..........	17	71	3	13	4	16	24	100
Ideation and imagery......	41	79	6	12	5	9	5°	100
Habits and experience......	24	75	3	9	5	16	32	100
Circumstances	4	57	1	16	2	27	7	100
Physical makeup . .	5	68	1	16	1	16	7	100
Total Personal . . .	109	73	17	11	23	16	149	100
Grand Total	219	72	37	12	49	16	305	100

Table xxx

Outcome in relation to Judge Baker Foundation prognosis

	Success		Temporary Success		Failure		Unknown		Total	
	Number	Per cent	Number	Per cent	Number	Per cent	Number	Per cent	Number	Per cent
Boys										
Good	96	58	55	33	15	9			166	100
Fair......................	39	40	37	37	20	20	3	3	99	100
Poor......................	24	25	31	32	37	39	4	4	96	100
Deferred..................	3	19	6	37	7	44			16	100
Conditional	10	56	4	22	4	22			18	100
None			2	40	2	40	1	20	5	100
Total	172	43	135	34	85	21	8	2	400	100
Girls										
Good	44	92	3	6	1	2			48	100
Fair......................	16	70	3	13	4	17			23	100
Poor......................	9	53	2	12	6	35			17	100
Deferred..................	4	67	2	33					6	100
Conditional	3	50	2	33	1	17			6	100
Total	76	76	12	12	12	12			100	100

TABLE XXXI

Outcome in relation to length of probation term

	Success		Temporary Success		Failure		Unknown		Total	
	Num-ber	Per cent	Num-ber	Per cent	Num-ber	Per cent	Num-ber	Per cent	Num-ber	Per cent
Boys										
Less than 6 months........	63	38.5	46	28	53	32.5	1	1	163	100
6 months to 1 year..........	67	52	50	38	13	10			130	100
1 year to 1 year 6 months....	31	46	27	40	9	13	1	1	68	100
1 year 6 months to 2 years..	6	28.5	9	43	6	28.5			21	100
2 years and over	5	28	3	17	4	22	6	33	18	100
Total	172	43	135	34	85	21	8	2	400	100
Girls										
Less than 6 months........	22	68.5	4	12.5	6	19			32	100
6 months to 1 year..........	34	85	5	12.5	1	2.5			40	100
1 year to 1 year 6 months....	10	72	2	14	2	14			14	100
1 year 6 months to 2 years..	7	78	1	11	1	11			9	100
2 years and over	3	60			2	40			5	100
Total	76	76	12	12	12	12			100	100

TABLE XXXII

Outcome in relation to companionship in offense

	Success		Temporary Success		Failure		Unknown		Total	
	Number	Per cent	Number	Per cent	Number	Per cent	Number	Per cent	Number	Per cent
BOYS										
Alone—acting on own initiative	35	34	26	25	39	37	4	4	104	100
Alone—acting on instigation of others	10	50	8	40	2	10			20	100
With one companion	22	51	1.1	26	10	23			43	100
With two or more companions	105	45	90	38	34	15	4	2	233	100
Total	172	43	135	34	85	21	8	2	400	100
GIRLS										
Alone—acting on own initiative	25	73	2	6	7	21			34	100
Alone—acting on instigation of others	15	75	4	20	1	5			20	100
With one companion	10	63	5	31	1	6			16	100
With two or more companions	26	87	1	3	3	10			30	100
Total	76	76	12	12	12	12			100	100

TABLE XXXIII

Outcome in relation to recreation classification

	Success		Temporary Success		Failure		Unknown		Total	
	Number	Per cent	Number	Per cent	Number	Per cent	Number	Per cent	Number	Per cent
BOYS										
Good	35	61	18	32	4	7			57	100
Fair.......................	46	41	39	34.5	25	22	3	2.5	113	100
Poor.......................	71	42	60	35.5	34	20	4	2.5	169	100
Vicious	20	33	18	29	22	36	1	2	61	100
Total	172	43	135	34	85	21	8	2	400	100
GIRLS										
Good	16	100							16	100
Fair.......................	27	77	5	14	3	9			35	100
Poor.........	23	82	4	14	1	4			28	100
Vicious	10	48	3	14	8	38			21	100
Total ....,	76	76	12	12	12	12			100	100

INDEX